life is a soap **bubble**

OSHO

Life is a soap bubble.
Those who don't see it like that are drowned and
destroyed in it. But those who become aware of this
truth start searching for a life which is eternal.

life is a soap **bubble**

100 Ways to Look at Life

Originally published in Hindi as *Path Ke Pradeep*, by Osho. These 100
letters were written by Osho, and mailed to a Yoga Sohan in connection with
events during a meditation camp in which she participated. Osho promised
her that he would send her a letter every day...and that she should keep
them so they could be published one day.
The complete OSHO text archive can be found via the online OSHO Library
at www.osho.com/Library

OSHO MEDIA INTERNATIONAL
New York • Zurich • Mumbai
an imprint of
OSHO INTERNATIONAL
www.osho.com/oshointernational

Library of Congress Catalog-In-Publication Data is available

Printed in India by Manipal Technologies Limited, Karnataka

ISBN: 978-1-938755-99-6
Also available as eBook: 978-0-88050-435-5

contents

preface

I would like you to remember: Live, and try to know what life is. Don't be bothered about death, heaven and hell, and this goddamned God. Simply remain with the life that is dancing in you, breathing in you, alive in you. You have to come closer to yourself to know it. Perhaps you are standing too far away from yourself; your concerns have taken you far away. You have to come back home.

So remember that while you are alive it is so precious – don't miss a single moment. Squeeze the whole juice of it, and that juice will give you the taste of the existential, and that will be a revelation of all that is hidden from you and will remain hidden from you.

Respect life, revere life. There is nothing more holy than life, nothing more divine than life. And life does not consist of big things. Those religious fools have been telling you, "Do big things," and life consists of small things. The strategy is clear. They tell you, "Do big things, something great, something that your name will be remembered for afterward. Do something great." And of course it appeals to the ego. The ego is the agent of the priest. All the churches and all the synagogues and all the temples have only one agent, and that is the ego. They don't use different agencies; there are no other agencies. There is only one agency and that is the ego – do something great, something big.

I want to tell you, there is nothing big, nothing great.

Life consists of very small things. So if you become interested in so-called big things, you will be missing life.

Life consists of sipping a cup of tea, of gossiping with a friend; going for a morning walk, not going anywhere in particular, just for a walk, no goal, no end, from any point you can turn back; cooking food for someone you love; cooking food for yourself because you love your body too; washing your clothes, cleaning the floor, watering the garden. These small things, very small things... Saying hello to a stranger, which was not needed at all because there was no question of any business with the stranger...

The man who can say hello to a stranger can also say hello to a flower, can also say hello to the tree, can sing a song to the birds. They sing every day and you have not bothered at all that someday you should return the call. Just small things, very small things.

Osho
From Unconsciousness to Consciousness

Man is born in slavery. We are born as slaves to ourselves. We come into this world imprisoned in chains of desire, held tight by those subtle chains.

We have been enslaved like this since birth. It is something given by nature; we don't have to do anything to earn it. Man simply finds he is a slave. Freedom has to be earned and only someone who struggles and strives for it will find it. For freedom, a price has to be paid. Nothing of value in life is ever free. This slavery which nature gave you is not a misfortune; it would be a misfortune only if we failed to win our freedom. There is nothing wrong in being born a slave, but it is definitely wrong to die as one. Unless you find inner freedom, nothing in life will have any meaning or fulfillment. You may have been given life, but if you remain trapped in a prison of desires, if you never know the free sky of awareness, then you will never know life. There is no difference at all between someone imprisoned in desire and a bird imprisoned in a cage. You only enter the world of real life when your awareness is freed from desire.

If you want to know truth, become a master of yourself. Victory over truth is not for someone who is defeated by their own self.

2

You have to be tireless and devoted in your pursuit of truth. You deserve to find truth only if you strive with every breath.

The desire for truth should not be just one among all your other desires. Someone who desires truth half-heartedly doesn't really desire it at all. The longing for truth has to be whole-hearted and total. When your heart thirsts for truth totally and completely, that very thirst becomes the path. Remember, a burning thirst for truth is itself the path to it. Prayer arises only when your being has an infinite thirst for truth, and your heart beats just to discover the unknown. When you live and breathe only for truth, then in that same silent yearning you take the first steps toward it. Only love – a love burning with thirst – deserves and has the right to truth.

Truth is one, but the doors to find it can be many. And if you become attached to the door itself, you will stop at the door. Then the door of truth will never open for you.

Truth is everywhere. Everything that is, is truth. It has infinite forms. It is just like beauty. Beauty manifests itself in many forms, but that does not mean that beauty itself is many different things. What glows in the stars at night, and what gives off fragrance in the flowers, and what shows in the eyes as love – are they different from each another? The forms may be different, but the very same essence is present in them all. But he who gets stuck at the form never comes to know the soul. And he who stops at the beautiful is never able to experience beauty itself. Likewise, those who get stuck with words will remain without the truth.

Those who know this, transform obstacles on the path into stepping stones. And for those who do not know this, even stepping stones will become obstacles.

4

Self-knowledge is the only knowledge there is. What possible value could there be in those who do not know themselves, knowing anything else?

Man's greatest difficulty is his ignorance about himself. Just as there is darkness underneath a lamp, similarly man is in darkness about the reality of his own self, his own soul. When we don't even know ourselves, it is not surprising if our whole life goes wrong. Without self-realization, life is like a boat whose captain is not in his senses, but just goes on rowing and steering the boat wherever. Self-awareness is the basic essential for bringing the right momentum and destination to your life. Before I can know what I am supposed to be, it is essential to know what I am. It is only after I know what I am, that I can lay the foundation for the future which is dormant in me. It is only after I know what I am, that the unborn in me can be born. If your life is to have any meaning, if your boat is to reach the shore of fulfillment, then your whole effort should be to know yourself, before knowing anything else. Only then can other knowledge be of any use. Otherwise, knowledge in the hands of the ignorant is just suicidal.

The first longing of knowing is to know the self. If there is darkness there, there is darkness everywhere. And if there is light there, then there is light everywhere.

Man has to become discontent with himself; only then does he move toward godliness. He who becomes content with himself destroys himself.

I teach discontent. I teach you to be discontented with just being a person. Human life is just a temporary stopover on the whole journey of life, not the final destination. And those who take it to be the final destination waste a priceless opportunity to rise beyond man. We are a midpoint in a long process of evolution. Our past was part of the journey and so is our future. Evolution does not end with us, it will transcend us also. This would be easy to understand if we really saw ourselves, because the proof is that we are incomplete and unfulfilled in every way. We have not reached the point where nature should stop. Evolution – if there is indeed evolution – cannot rest before achieving godliness. There can be no meaningful end to evolution, nor any purpose or significance, without experiencing the totality of godliness.

Man is the path to reach godliness. And those who forgo the destination and are satisfied with just the path are indeed unfortunate! We have left the animal behind, and we have to move forward to reach godliness. We are just a bridge between the animal and godliness. That is why I lay so much emphasis on transcending man. We have to leave man behind, just as a snake sheds its skin and moves on. To transcend the state of man is the right use of your life. Other than that, everything else is a misuse. A path is not for stopping on. Its significance lies in going beyond it.

Don't just stop at how you find yourself now. This is

not the end of the path, but only its beginning. Understand that you have not reached the end of the path until you have become whole.

Stop worrying about darkness and turn on the light. People who think only about darkness can never find light.

6

There is a lot of darkness in life. And also evil and immorality. Some people resign themselves to this darkness and then their inner urge to reach the light, to find light, gradually becomes weaker and weaker. I call this resignation to darkness, the greatest sin. This is a crime which man commits against himself. All crimes against others come from this basic crime against yourself. Always remember that a person who doesn't do this to himself can't commit a sin against anyone else either. In an effort to avoid this darkness, some people become preoccupied with denying it. Then their life becomes just an ongoing fight to deny darkness. This is also a mistake. The person who resigns himself to darkness is mistaken and so is someone who fights it. You don't have to be resigned to darkness, nor do you have to fight it. Both are ignorance. The intelligent man does what he can to bring light. Darkness has no existence of its own; it is merely an absence of light. The moment light arrives, darkness disappears. It is the same with evil, immorality and irreligiousness. We don't have to wipe out evil, immorality and irreligiousness; it is enough to simply light the lamp of goodness, morality and religiousness. The light of religiousness is the death of irreligiousness.

Fighting darkness is fighting with an absence. This is insanity. If you have to fight, then fight for light to come. He who has light destroys darkness involuntarily.

7 The truth of life is found through balance and harmony. Those who go to the extreme in any direction wander away from the path.

The mind always swings and functions in extremes. It is very easy for it to swing from one extreme to the other; that is its nature. Someone who is very attached to his body can also, in reaction, be very harsh and cruel to his body. The same attachment is hidden there in this harshness and cruelty. He is still attached to his body, just as he was before, but now in exactly the opposite way. The body was the focus of attention before and it is the focus of attention now. To keep its original attitude of attachment, the mind deceives us by swinging to the other extreme. This is why the mind always functions in extremes. This attitude of the mind of moving to opposite extremes, I call disharmony. So what do I call harmony? I call it finding a middle point between two extremes and being stable at that midpoint. And where there is inner harmony, life is full of music. The music of life is the product of inner harmony. By finding and settling in the midpoint between love and hate of the body, inner harmony is found – which is beyond attachment and repulsion. By finding and settling in the midpoint between infatuation and disillusion with the world, the balance called sannyas is found. Whoever practices this balance between all the extremes goes beyond them, and the music of enlightenment enters his life. Man's mind lives on extremes, and it dies if there are no extremes. When the noise of the mind disappears, man spontaneously starts hearing the music that has always been playing inside him. This music of the self is enlightenment, is ultimate liberation, is the ultimate reality.

To throw yourself into flames of fire to escape drowning is no way to save yourself.

8

On a pitch-dark night, even a single ray of light is a blessing because if you follow it, you will reach the source of the light.

For some reason, a king became angry with his prime minister and imprisoned him in a cell at the top of a very tall minaret. This was actually a very painful death sentence, because no food was sent to him and there was no possibility of escape by jumping from the sky-high minaret.

When the prime minister was being taken to his prison, people noticed that he didn't look at all worried or unhappy. On the contrary, he was his usual cheerful self. His wife, bidding him a tearful farewell, asked why he was looking so cheerful. He said, "If even just a very thin thread of silk can be sent to me, I will get free. Won't you be able to do such a small thing?"

The wife thought about it a lot, but she could not figure out how to get the silk thread to him in that tall minaret. She asked a mystic. The mystic said, "Catch one of those insects called a *bhringa*. Tie a silk thread to its feet and put a drop of honey on its antenna. Then release it on the minaret with its head pointing upward."

She did that the same night. Lured by the scent of honey, slowly, slowly, the insect started to climb the minaret. Finally it completed its long journey and one end of the silk thread fell into the hands of the prisoner.

This thin silk thread became the means to his life and freedom because later, through this same thread, first a little thicker cotton thread was sent to him, then a thin rope was sent, and finally a thick rope. And with the help of the rope he managed to escape from the prison.

That's why I say that to reach the sun, even a single ray of light is enough. And you don't even need anyone to send you this ray. Everyone has it already. Those who can find this ray will also find the sun.

The life which is inside of man is a ray of immortality; the awareness inside is a drop of enlightenment; and the inner joy is nothing but a glimpse of *sat-chit-anand* – truth, consciousness, bliss.

9

What is prayer? Love and surrender. Where there is no love, there is no prayer. Let me tell you a wonderful story about love.

Noori, Rakkam, and a few other Sufi mystics, were charged with being infidels and sentenced to death. When the executioner came in front of Rakkam with a naked sword, Noori got up and, with great courtesy and happiness, put himself before the executioner in place of his friend.

The spectators were astonished. There was a crowd of thousands and a chill wave of silence swept through it. The executioner said, "Young man! A sword is not something you should be so anxious and eager to meet. It is not your turn yet."

And do you know what the mystic Noori replied? He said, "Love is my only religion. I know that in this world, life is the most valuable thing, but compared to love it is nothing. For someone who finds love, life is nothing more than a play.

"In the world, life is supreme. But love is even higher than life because it does not belong to the world, it belongs to truth. And love says that when death comes, put yourself in front of your friends, and when life is given, put yourself behind. This is what we call prayer."

Prayer cannot have any structure. It is a spontaneous outpouring of the heart. Just as a spring flows from a mountain, prayer flows from a heart full of love.

Everyone is a mirror. From morning till evening, this mirror gathers dust. And those who allow this dust to settle are no longer a mirror. As your mirror is, so is your awareness. The truth reflected in it is only truth to the extent that it is a mirror.

Someone once complained to a mystic that he was very disturbed by the stream of his thoughts. The mystic sent him to another mystic friend of his to sort out his problem. While seeing him off the mystic said, "Go, and watch very closely all the daily activities of my friend. From that, you will find a way out."

The man went. The mystic he had been sent to was an innkeeper. For a few days the man watched all his activities, but didn't notice anything special, anything worth learning. This mystic was just a very ordinary person. There were no signs of wisdom in him. Certainly he was simple and had a childlike innocence, but there seemed nothing special in his behavior.

The man observed all the daily activities of the mystic very closely. The only thing he couldn't see was what he did just before going to sleep and when he got up in the morning. When asked, the mystic said, "Nothing much. At night I wash all the used utensils. And because a little dust settles on them during the night, I wash them again in the morning. The utensils should never have any dirt or dust – it is important to remember this. You see, I am the innkeeper of this inn."

The man returned to his master very disappointed. He told his master about all the daily activities of the mystic and everything that had happened between them.

His master said, "You saw and heard everything that was worth learning, but you weren't able to understand. You should also clean your mind at night and then wash it anew in the morning. Slowly, slowly, your mind will become completely free of dirt. It is absolutely essential for an innkeeper to stay aware of this."

Daily cleaning of the mind is essential. The freshness and cleanliness of your life depends entirely on whether or not your mind has been cleaned. And those who ignore this do so at their own peril.

The eternal is hidden in the moment, and the vastness **11** of infinity is contained in the atom. He who ignores the atom, thinking it is just an atom, loses the infinite itself. It is only by digging in the lowest that you find the highest.

Each and every moment of life is significant. And no moment is less or more valuable than any other moment. To wait for a particular moment to find bliss is useless. Those who are aware turn each and every moment into bliss. And those who keep waiting for the right opportunity lose the very opportunity of life itself. The fulfillment of life is not attained all in one go, in a lump sum. It is to be found bit by bit, in each and every moment.

Once, after a master left his body, his disciples were asked, "What did your master value most?"

They replied, "Anything that he was involved in, in any given moment."

The ocean is made up of many single drops. And life consists of many individual moments. He who becomes aware of the drop comes to know the whole ocean. And he who has experienced the moment has experienced the whole of life.

12 There is no bigger mistake than the idea of "I." It is the biggest obstacle on the path to truth. Those who don't overcome this obstacle will never make any progress on the path of truth.

A sannyasin was passing through a village. A sannyasin friend of his was in the same village, so he thought he would visit him before moving on. Although it was nearly midnight, he went to meet him. Seeing a light shining, he knocked on the window. A voice came from inside, "Who is it?"

Thinking that his voice would be enough to identify him, he simply replied, "It is I."

But no answer came from inside. He knocked on the window many times, but there was no reply. He began to wonder if the house was empty.

He said loudly, "Friend, why aren't you opening the door for me. Why don't you reply?"

A voice was heard from inside: "Who is this fool who is calling himself 'I'? Except for God, nobody has the right to say 'I.'"

Our "I" is the only lock on the door to truth. If you break that lock, suddenly you realize that the door was always open.

Truth exists within our very self. And it is not even so difficult to find, but we have to travel inside to do so. When someone goes inside himself, he finds truth as well as himself, at the deepest core of his life's breath.

In the Second World War, a badly wounded French soldier was found at a railway station. There were so many wounds on his face that it was difficult to make out who he was. Identifying him was made even more difficult by a wound he had received to his forehead, which had made him forget who he was. He had lost his memory.

When questioned, he would say, "I don't know who I am, or where I come from," and a stream of tears would start flowing from his eyes. In the end, three families claimed he belonged to them. Of course, it was not possible that he belonged to three families, so they took him to each of the three towns and left him on his own.

In two of the towns he just stood, very confused, and didn't know what to do. But when he arrived at the third town, his dull eyes suddenly lit up and his expressionless face started showing emotion. He went to one street all by himself and, seeing a particular house, started to run toward it. It was as if some power had suddenly entered his sleepy soul. He had recognized something; he had remembered his home. With a feeling of utter joy he said, "This is my house. Now I remember who I am!"

The same thing has happened to all of us. We have forgotten who we are because we have forgotten where our home is. Once we are able to see our home, it is natural to recognize our true self.

Someone who keeps on wandering outside will never reach the town where his real home is. And if he doesn't arrive there, he cannot find his self. Not only on the outside, but on the inside too, there is a journey which takes you to your self and to the truth.

Choosing between truth and the self: if you choose truth, **14**
not only will you find truth, but you will also find your
true self. And if you choose the self, you will lose both.

Man has to lose his self before becoming the truth.
The self is a veil covering the truth. That very way of
looking, that attitude of seeing the world from the point
of "I," is the hindrance. It is only this I-sight, nothing else,
which separates him from the truth. Man's becoming an
I was his fall from godliness. It is the material nature of I
that makes him fall, and in losing the I, he rises to the
immaterial and to the state of godliness. The I means
falling down. No-I means rising up. So, what appears to
be losing is actually not losing – it is a gain. The existence of the I that you have to lose is not actually an
existence, but a dream. What you will find by losing it is
the truth.

Only when the seed completely loses itself in the
earth can it sprout and become a tree.

15 Life is an art. It is not just about living somehow or other. Only he who lives with a purpose actually lives.

What is the meaning of life? What is the point of our existence? What is the purpose? What is it that we want to become and to attain? If you have no awareness of a destination, how can any step be right? And if you have no destination, how can you have total fulfillment or contentment?

He who has no awareness of the meaning of a total life is like someone who has flowers and wants to make a garland of them, but doesn't have a thread to join them together. Eventually he will see that the flowers can't be made into a garland, and there is no direction or sense of wholeness in his life.

All his experiences will be fragmentary and won't give rise to the energy which becomes true knowing. He will remain without that total experience where living, or not living, is one and the same. His life will be like a tree which never produces flowers or fruits. He will know happiness and suffering, but will never taste bliss because bliss arises only after life is experienced in its totality.

If you want to find bliss, then make your life a garland of flowers. String all the experiences of your life with the thread of a single purpose. Someone who does not do that will not find the meaning and fulfillment of life.

If you long for truth, don't tie your mind down with any **16** ideology. Truth never comes where there is ideology. Truth and ideology are enemies.

In the search for truth, a free and open inquiry is the first step. And he who burdens his mind with any kind of doctrine or ideology before experiencing it for himself will cripple and block his inquiry. Inquiry is the momentum and life force of the search. It is only through inquiry that intelligence awakens and consciousness rises. But inquiry is born from doubt, not from faith. That's why I consider doubt, not faith, to be an essential tool for the traveler on the path of truth. Doubt is a sign of healthy thinking and only when it is used properly do the veils covering truth start falling away. A moment comes when truth is revealed. Understand clearly that both believers and non-believers are essentially men of faith. Faith is both negative and positive. Doubt is a third, altogether different, state of mind. It is neither believing nor not-believing. It is a freedom to inquire, independent of both.

How can people who are already tied down to certain ideologies go on the search for truth? Only the boats of those who untie the chains of belief and non-belief from the anchors of ideologies can sail into the ocean of truth.

To find the truth, total freedom of mind is needed. He whose mind is dependent on some doctrine will not be able to see the sun of truth.

17 If your eyes are open, then everything in life is a school of learning. And if you have a hunger to learn, you will learn from every person and every situation. And remember, if you don't learn this way, you cannot learn anything in life. Emerson has said, "Every man I meet is better than I am in some point, and in that I learn from him."

I remember a story:

In Mecca, a barber was giving someone a haircut. Just then, the Sufi mystic Junnaid came in and said, "In the name of Allah, will you shave me also?"

The minute he heard the word *Allah*, the barber said to his customer: "Friend, now I can't shave you. You see, in Allah's name, I should first take care of this mystic. Allah comes first." Then he shaved the mystic with great love and devotion. He bowed to him, and the mystic took his leave.

A few days later, when someone had given him some money, Junnaid went back to the barber to pay him, but the barber would not accept the money. He said, "Don't you feel ashamed? You asked me to shave you in the name of Allah, not for money!"

For the rest of his life, the Sufi mystic would tell his companions, "I learned selfless devotion to God from a barber."

Great messages lie hidden even in the most insignificant thing. Someone who knows how to uncover them finds wisdom. By living his life with awareness, each experience becomes part of his intelligence. Those who remain unconscious turn away even the splendor that may knock at their door.

18   Man's feet are pointing toward hell and his head toward heaven. Heaven and hell are both his potential. Which of these two seeds bears fruit is entirely up to him.

Man's greatness lies entirely in his own hands; nature has merely given him possibilities. His outcome is not predetermined. He creates his own self by himself. This freedom is a splendor, but if we want, we can also make it a calamity. For most people, this freedom ends up as a misfortune because in the very potential to create, the potential and freedom to destroy lie hidden. And most people make use of the second alternative because destruction is easier than creation. What could be easier than to destroy yourself? To destroy yourself, it is enough simply not to be self-creative. Nothing other than that is needed. If someone is not soaring upward in life, he unknowingly and unintentionally starts falling back and down.

I have heard...

Once a group was discussing whether man is the greatest of all living creatures because he can control all the other species. But some were of the opinion that man is even lower than dogs because they have much more self-control than man. Hussain happened to be present at this debate and both sides asked him to cast the decisive vote. Hussain said, "I will tell you what I think and then you can draw your own conclusions. As long as I use my mind and my life in noble deeds, I am nearer the gods. But when my mind and my life become sinful, even a dog is greater than a thousand Hussains."

Man is a combination of the mortal and the immortal. He who is a slave to the body and its desires will continue to fall. And he who is intent on his search for the immortal will reach *sat-chit-anand* – truth, consciousness, bliss – and ultimately that's what he himself will become.

19 Life is attained only by knowing what is inside you. Someone who does not know that will always be surrounded by
death and the fear of death.

Once, a sannyasin was asked by some of his friends,
"If some wicked people attack you, what will you do?"
He said, "I will enter my fortress within and sit there."
His enemies heard about this.
One day, his enemies surrounded him in an aban-
doned place and said, "Now sir, please tell us, where is
that fortress of yours?"
The sannyasin laughed heartily and then, putting his
hand on his heart, said, "This is my fortress. Nobody can
ever attack it. The body can be destroyed, but never what
is within it. That is my fort. My security lies in knowing
the way to it."
For someone who doesn't know that this fort exists,
his whole life is insecure. He who doesn't know this fort
will always be surrounded by enemies his whole life.
He has not yet found a refuge of peace and security.
Those who look for this place on the outside look in vain
because it happens to be inside.

You only start knowing life when you are settled in
your own being; beyond that point, only death exists.

Only those who have no needs are wealthy. Desires make you poor and a mind besieged by desires becomes a beggar. It is continuously asking for something or other. You are wealthy only if you have no demands left.

The great sage Kanad got his name because he used to live on the *kana*, the particles of grain left on the ground after the peasants had reaped their harvest. Who could be poorer than that?

The king of the country heard about his suffering. He sent his minister with an abundance of wealth and provisions for him. When the minister arrived, the great sage said to him, "I am well provided for. Distribute this wealth amongst those who need it."

This happened three times. Finally the king himself came to see the sage, bringing much wealth with him. He asked the sage to accept it, but he said, "Give it to those who don't have anything. Look, I have everything I need." The king looked. He wondered how a man who had nothing except a loincloth on his body could say he had everything!

When he returned, he told the whole story to his queen. She said, "You have made a mistake. You should not go to a sage to give him something; you should go to receive something. Only those who have something inside can renounce everything outside."

The king went back to see the great sage the same night and asked to be forgiven.

Kanad said to him, "Look who is poor! Look at me and then look at yourself – not outside, but inside. I do not ask for anything, I do not desire anything, and that's why I have spontaneously become an emperor."

There is a wealth outside, but there is also a wealth inside. What is outside gets taken away sooner or later. That is why those who know do not call it wealth, but rather disaster. Their search is for what is inside. Once found, it can never be lost. This is the only real attainment. With other things, even when you have them, the demand for more never ends. But once you have found the inner wealth, nothing else is left to attain.

Those who seek God as some kind of object or thing are clearly ignorant. It is not a thing. It is a name for the ultimate experience of light, bliss, and deathlessness. It is also not a person you can find somewhere outside. It is simply the ultimate refinement of your own consciousness.

21

Somebody once asked a mystic, "If there is a God, then why isn't it visible?"

The mystic said: "God is not an object, but an experience. There is no way to see it; but to experience it, yes, there definitely is." But this did not seem to satisfy the inquirer. His eyes showed that the question was still lingering in him. Seeing this, the mystic picked up a big stone that was lying nearby and hit his leg with it. This made a large wound in his leg, and blood started gushing out.

The man asked, "What have you done? That must be very painful. What type of madness is this?"

The mystic started laughing and said, "Pain is not visible and yet it exists. Love cannot be seen and yet it exists. God is also like that."

Not only that which is visible exists, the invisible also exists. And the invisible is more profound than the visible because to experience it you have to dive into the depths of your own being. Only then are you receptive enough to be able to touch it and experience it. To know it, not ordinary eyes, but a profound sensitivity of experiencing must be attained. Only then is it revealed. Having found it, nothing else remains to be found. And only then do you understand that it is not something outside that can be seen; it is inside, it is hidden in the seer himself.

God is not to be sought out, but dug out. Those who go on digging within themselves ultimately experience it as the original source, and the ultimate flowering of their own being.

Remember, unawareness is the only thing I call a sin. In an aware state of consciousness, sin is as impossible as putting your hand knowingly and consciously into a fire. He who has learned the art of awareness, spontaneously becomes religious.

There is an incident from the life of the mystic Bheekan. One night, he was delivering a discourse. One of the listeners, Aso, was sitting asleep in the first row. Bheekan said to him, "Aso, are you sleeping?"

Aso opened his eyes and replied: "No, venerable one, never." After a while he went back to sleep again.

Bheekan again asked him, "Aso! Are you sleeping?"

Again he got the same reply: "No, venerable one, never." When has someone drowned in sleep ever told the truth? And even if he wanted to, how could he?

Once again, sleep descended on Aso. But what Bheekan asked this time was really astonishing. There are many meanings to it. Everyone should ask himself this question; it alone is the root of all metaphysical thinking. He asked loudly, "Aso, are you alive?" Of course, Aso was asleep. In his sleep, he must have thought it was the same question again. In his sleep, the words *sleeping* and *alive* must have sounded similar!

Rubbing his eyes, he replied: "No, venerable one, never." By mistake, the right answer slipped out.

Someone who is asleep is the same as dead. What possible difference can there be between death, and a life of unawareness and inertia? Only the awake are alive. And unless we wake in awareness and intelligence, we are not yet alive.

He who wants to attain to life will have to throw off sleepiness and unconsciousness. Generally we are asleep and all our feelings, thoughts, and actions are unconscious. We perform them as if someone else is making us do them, as if we are doing them in deep hypnosis. To be awake means that nothing your mind and body do is done unconsciously – whatever is done, is done with full awareness and alertness. When this happens, bad becomes impossible and good happens spontaneously.

When the morning dawns, I accept the morning and when the evening comes, I accept the evening. Light has its own bliss, and darkness also has its own bliss. After I understood this, I have never known any unhappiness.

A mystic left his monastery. When he returned, he learned that his only son had died and the funeral procession had just left. He was mad with sorrow. Why wasn't he told? Blind with rage, he ran toward the cremation grounds.

When he caught up with the funeral procession, his master was walking beside the dead body. He ran and clutched the master; he was almost unconscious with sorrow. Then he asked him, "Please give me a few words of consolation. I am going mad."

The master said, "Why words? Know the truth itself. There is no greater consolation than that." And lifting the lid of the casket, the master said. "See! See what is."

He saw. His tears stopped. The dead body lay in front of him; he kept looking at it and an insight dawned in him: what is, is. What is there to laugh or cry about? If life is a reality, so death is a reality. What is, is. To want it to be otherwise is to create unhappiness.

Once I was very ill. The doctors were afraid, and there was deep anguish in the eyes of near and dear ones. And I was really feeling like laughing because I was very eager to experience death. Death did not come, but I experienced a truth: whatever we accept cannot make us unhappy.

24

I was accompanying a funeral procession and I said to the people there: "You are blind if you do not see this as your own funeral procession. As far as I am concerned, I am seeing myself in place of that dead body, all wrapped up. Alas! If you could only see like that too, your whole life would be different."

The focus of he who has known his own death shifts from the world to truth.

Sheik Sadi has written:

A long time ago, on the shores of Dajla, the skull of a corpse spoke to a traveler. It said, "O beloved, walk with a little more care! Once upon a time I had a royal kingdom and wore a crown. Victory followed my every step and I walked as if my feet were on air. I was lost in this unconsciousness. Then suddenly one day it all came to an end. Worms have eaten me away and every foot that passes this way kicks me. Pull the cotton wool of unawareness from your ears, so that you can receive the teaching coming from the voice of the dead."

What is that teaching coming from the voice of the dead? And do we ever hear it? He who hears it, his life will be transformed.

Death is joined with birth. What lies between birth and death is not life, but merely an appearance of life. How can it be life because life cannot die? Birth has an end, but not life. And death has a beginning, but life doesn't. Life is beyond both. Those who don't know this are not alive, even though they may be living. And those who have known it do not die even after death.

Until you have freed yourself from the mechanical flow of thoughts, sitting in temples and places of worship has no value whatsoever, and the prayer beads you hold in your hands are all false.

He who becomes free of the waves of thoughts is a temple wherever he happens to be, and whatever work he is doing is a prayer.

Someone once said to a mystic, "My wife doesn't have any faith in the pursuit of religion. If you could please make her understand, that would be very nice."

The next morning, the mystic went to the man's house. He found the wife outside in the garden. The mystic asked about her husband and she replied, "As far as I know, at this moment he must be quarreling in some cobbler's shop!"

It was still the mistiness of pre-dawn; the husband was busy with his prayer beads in the adjacent temple. He could not tolerate such a blatant lie. He immediately came out and said, "That is absolutely false. I was in my temple."

Even the mystic was surprised, but the wife said, "Were you really in the temple? The rosary was in your hands, your body was in the temple, but wasn't your mind somewhere else?"

The husband came to his senses. True, while using the rosary he had gone to the cobbler's shop. He had to buy shoes and he had told his wife the night before that he would go and buy them first thing in the morning. And in his thoughts he had started bargaining and quarreling over the price of shoes!

Let go of thoughts, be without thoughts, then where-ever you are, God will be there for you. Where will you go to look for it? And how will you search for something you do not even know? It is found not by searching for it, but by creating peace in yourself. Up until now, no one has ever gone to it, rather it comes on its own to whoever invites it in the right way. It is futile to go to the temple. Those who know become temples themselves.

"Who am I?" The doors of wisdom will remain closed to anyone who does not ask himself this question. It is the only key to open that door. Ask yourself, "Who am I?" He who asks this question with intensity and totality will receive the answer from within himself.

Carlyle had become old; his body had seen eighty springs. The body that was once very beautiful and healthy had now become dilapidated and loose: signs of old age were clearly visible. This is an incident from one morning in his old age.

Carlyle was in the bathroom. As he was drying his body after his bath, it suddenly struck him that the body he had known as his, had long since gone! His body had changed completely. Where was the body he had loved so much? The body he had felt so proud of was now left in ruins. But at the same time, he had a completely new awareness: "Though the body is no longer the same, I am still the same. I have not changed." Then he asked himself, "Ah! Then who the devil am I?"

Everyone has to ask themselves this very question. This is the real question; it is the question of all questions. Those who don't ask this question don't really ask anything. Those who don't even ask, how can they expect an answer?

Ask – let this question echo and reverberate in your innermost depths: "Who am I?" When someone asks with all their life force, he definitely gets the answer. And that answer changes the whole direction and meaning of his life. Before that, man is blind. Only after that can he see.

27 Even a single ray of truth is enough. Just a glimpse of truth does what the weight of all the scriptures cannot do. Even huge volumes of scriptures about light will not help bring light into darkness; you just need to light a small lamp.

An old washerwoman was always seen in the audience of Ralph Waldo Emerson's lectures. People were very surprised to see her there – what would a poor illiterate woman make of Emerson's serious talks? Finally, someone asked her what she understood.

The reply that old washerwoman gave was really astonishing. She said, "How can I tell you about what I don't understand? I have understood one thing quite well, but I don't know if others have understood it or not. I am illiterate, but that one thing is quite enough for me – it has changed my entire life. What is it? It is that even I, a poor illiterate woman, am not far from God. God is near. Not only near, is actually inside us. I have understood this small truth, and now I can't imagine that there could be any greater truth than this!"

Life is transformed not through knowing lots of facts, but rather through even just a small experience of truth. Those who busy themselves with trying to know a lot, often find themselves without that tiny spark of truth that brings real transformation, and which reveals new dimensions of wisdom in life.

I have heard that Christ raised the dead from their graves **28**
and gave them life. A man who thinks himself to be only
the body is in the grave, nowhere else. Only when he
realizes that the soul is higher than the body does he rise
from the grave and start to live.

In an ancient monastery in Egypt, a monk had died.
He was lowered into a crypt built deep underground. But,
fortunately or unfortunately, he was not dead and after
a while he regained consciousness in that place of the
dead. It is difficult to even imagine his mental pain and
anguish. In that dark place filled with death and stench,
where hundreds of corpses were rotting, he was alive!
No way to get out, not even the slightest chance of any
sound reaching outside.

What did he do? Did he die, thirsty and hungry? Did
he let go of his attachment to this almost worse-than-dead
life and not try to save himself? No, friend, the lust for life
is very deep and intense. The monk started living in those
surroundings. He ate worms and insects. He would drink
the filthy water dripping from the walls of the crypt and
survived on worms. He took clothes from the dead bod-
ies and used them for his own clothing and bed. And he
would pray constantly that one of his colleagues would
die, because only when somebody died would the doors
of his dark home open.

Years passed. For him, all track of time was lost. Then
one day somebody died and the doors opened, and he
was found alive. His beard had turned white and was so
long that it reached the ground. But when he was pulled
out of the crypt, he remembered to take with him the pile

of clothes he had gathered from the corpses and the coins he had collected from their pockets.

Is this something that happened in the past, or is it a reflection of our own lives? Isn't this situation happening in the lives of all of us, now and here? When I look, I find that each of us is praying for the death of one another. And we are all living in a place of corpses from where there is no visible exit. We too are grabbing clothes and money from other corpses and survive on worms and insects. And all this is happening because of our blind lust for life.

A man driven by blind lust for life cannot experience real life. Only he who is free of this mist knows life. Know well that a consciousness driven by this is simply in the grave, nowhere else.

To a flower, the whole world is a flower. And to thorns, it is thorns. Others appear to be what you yourself are. How is it possible to see something in others which is not already in you?

We may wander all over the earth in search of beauty, but if it is not inside ourselves, it is impossible to find it anywhere else.

A stranger arrived in a village. He asked an old man sitting at the entry to the village, "Are the folks of this village nice and friendly?"

Instead of answering the question directly, the old man asked the stranger, "Friend, what are the people like where you come from?"

The stranger replied sadly and angrily, "Very cruel, nasty and unjust. They alone are responsible for all my problems. But why are you asking me this?"

The old man remained silent for some time and then said, "Friend, I am very sorry, the people here are also the same. You will find them the same."

Hardly had the stranger left than another traveler arrived and asked the old man the same question: "What type of people live here?"

The old man said, "Friend, first can you tell me what the people are like where you come from?"

Hearing this, the stranger became full of fond memories and his eyes moistened with tears of joy. He said, "Ah! Very loving and very kind. They were the sole cause of all my joys. I wish I never had to leave them!"

The old man said, "Friend, the folks here are also very loving. You will not find them any less kind here, they too are like your folks. There is not much difference between people."

The world is a mirror. What we see in others is nothing but our own reflection. Until someone is able to see goodness and beauty in everyone, he should know that there is still some shortcoming in him.

It is futile to try and take darkness away from life because darkness cannot be taken away. Those who know do not try to get rid of darkness; they simply light a lamp.

There is an ancient folklore – it relates to the time when man had no light, no fire, when nights were a great suffering. People thought of all sorts of ways to get rid of the darkness, but none of them worked. Somebody said, "Recite mantras," so mantras were recited. Somebody suggested praying, so people raised their hands to the empty sky and prayed. But the darkness didn't go away; it remained.

Finally, a young thinker and inventor said, "Let's put the darkness in baskets and bury it in the ground. In this way, the darkness will gradually become weaker and eventually there will be none left." It seemed very logical, so the people spent many nights filling baskets with darkness and emptying them into trenches. But when they looked, they found nothing there. They became bored and fed up with it, but by this time throwing away darkness had become a custom, so each person went on burying at least one basket of darkness every night.

Then a young man fell in love with a fairy and they got married. On the very first night, the elderly folks of the house asked the bride to throw at least one basket of darkness into the trench. Hearing this, the fairy laughed. Then she made a wick out of some white material, poured butter into an earthen bowl and rubbed two stones together. The people were struck dumb with what they saw – fire had been made, the lamp was burning, and the darkness had receded into the distance! From that day on, the people stopped trying to bury the darkness because they had learned how to light a lamp.

But when it comes to life, most of us still don't know how to light a lamp, and instead waste an opportunity by fighting with darkness – the opportunity that could have been transformed into divine light.

Fill yourself with the longing to find godliness, and darkness will leave you all by itself. If you keep fighting with darkness, you keep sinking deeper and deeper into it. Make life a positive ascendance, not a negative escape. This is the golden key to success.

We have treated life like a man who has shut his eyes to the sun. So is it surprising that our feet stumble into ditches? Keeping our eyes shut is the only sin or crime. The moment we open our eyes, all darkness disappears.

I am reminded of a sannyasin. He was severely tortured, but it did not destroy his peace. Great suffering was inflicted on him, but no one could destroy his bliss. Even in the midst of torture he remained happy, and his voice was full of sweetness in response to all the abuse. Someone asked him, "How did you get such supernatural power?"

He said, "Supernatural? Where? There is nothing supernatural about it. It is just that I have learned how to use my eyes. I am no longer a blind person with eyes."

But what is the connection between eyes and peace, saintliness and tolerance? The person he was speaking to couldn't understand. To help him understand, the sannyasin repeated: "When I look up at the sky, I realize that life on earth is very fleeting and dreamlike. So how can the behavior of people who are in a dream touch me? When I look inside myself, I find that what is eternal and indestructible cannot be harmed by anyone in any way.

"And when I look around me, I find there are so many hearts that love me and have kindness and love for me, even though I do not deserve their love. Seeing all this, a feeling of deep joy and gratitude arises in my heart. And when I look behind me, I find so many people who are in pain and suffering that my heart becomes full of love and compassion. So I am in peace and gratitude;

I am blissful and have become full of love. I have learned to make use of my eyes, dear friend. I am not blind."

And what a great power it is not to be blind! To use your eyes is what saintliness is all about. That is what religiousness is.

Eyes are there for seeing the truth. Wake up – and see. He who has eyes, but keeps them shut, sows the seeds of his own misery.

In life, revolution toward truth happens very fast. Even if **32** just an insight into truth is there, changes happen simultaneously, not gradually. The horizontal exists only where there is no self-awareness; otherwise life is transformed vertically, in a leap, like a flash of lightning.

Some people once brought a man to see me. He had acquired a bad habit and his loved ones wanted him to drop it as it was destroying his life. I asked him, "What do you think?"

He said, "Slowly, slowly, I will give it up."

Hearing this, I started laughing and said to him: "Giving up slowly doesn't mean anything. If you fell into a fire, would you come out slowly? And if you said you would try to come out gradually, what would that mean? Wouldn't it show clearly that you couldn't see the fire?"

Then I told him a story:

A wealthy young man was very influenced by sitting close to Paramahansa Ramakrishna. One day, he brought a thousand gold coins to offer him. Ramakrishna said, "Go and offer this rubbish to the Ganges." Now what could he do? He had to go and throw them into the Ganges. But he took a very long time to return because he was counting each and every coin before throwing it! One... Two... Three... One thousand – naturally it took him a long time. Hearing about this, Ramakrishna said to him, "Where you could have reached with a single step, you unnecessarily took a thousand steps."

If you have known and experienced the truth, you don't have to renounce anything gradually. The very experience of truth becomes renunciation. Where igno-rance cannot reach even through a thousand steps, experience reaches in a single step.

33

If someone achieves everything by losing his self in the bargain, he has made a very costly deal. He has given away diamonds in exchange for stones. A man who has managed to keep his self, even if he had to lose everything, is more intelligent.

Once, a very rich man's mansion caught fire. With the help of his servants, he very carefully got everything out of the house. Chairs, tables, wardrobes full of clothes, account books and ledgers, safes – and everything else that was in the house. Meanwhile, the fire spread all over the house. The owner was standing outside with everyone else. Dazed, with tears in his eyes, he watched his beloved home being reduced to ashes. Finally, he asked the servants, "Has anything been left inside?"

They replied, "No, but just to make sure we'll go inside and have another look."

When they went in, they found their master's only son lying in his room. The room was almost completely burned by the fire and the son was dead. Shocked at the sight, they rushed out, beating their chests and weeping bitterly, crying, "Oh, what fools we were! In trying to save the belongings of the house, we totally overlooked and forgot about the master of those belongings. We have saved the things, but lost the master to whom all this belongs."

Doesn't this ring true for each and every one of us? Won't we all one day have to say the same thing, "What a pity! While I was busy trying to save who knows what, worthless things, I have lost the master of those things – I have lost my own self." There is no bigger calamity than this in man's life, but there are very few blessed people who manage to avoid it.

Remember that there is nothing higher than your own self. He who attains that, attains everything. And he who loses that, whatever else he may have gained is of no value at all.

The bliss in life lies in your attitude. It is in you. It is up to you. It is not in what you get, but rather in how you see it. That is where it is hidden.

I have heard...

Somewhere, a temple was being built. Three laborers were breaking stones in the sun and a traveler asked them, "What are you doing?"

The first man replied, "I am breaking stones." He had not said anything wrong, but in the way he said it, there was a sense of burden and suffering in his voice. Certainly, how can breaking stones be a joyful experience? Having answered, he continued to break stones with a heavy heart.

The traveler looked at the second man, who replied, "I am earning my living." And what he said was also true. But although he did not look sad, there was no feeling of joy in his eyes either. Clearly, earning your living is work, and how can there be any joy in it?

He looked at the third man who was singing a song. He stopped his singing and said, "I am building a temple." There was a shine in his eyes and a song in his heart. To be creating a temple is certainly a blessed feeling! And what greater joy can there be than in creating?

These three answers hold true about life also. Which one you choose depends entirely on you. And the meaning and significance of your life depends on which one you choose. Life is the same, but everything changes with different attitudes. With different attitudes, flowers become thorns and thorns become flowers.

Bliss is everywhere, but not everyone has the heart

needed to experience it. And no one has ever found bliss until he has first prepared his heart to experience it. It is not about having a special place or circumstances, rather, he who attains to the right state of feeling to experience bliss, finds bliss under every circumstance and in every place.

Who in this world does not want peace? But people are not aware of it and they don't look for sources which will give peace. Our inner being longs for peace, but everything we do just adds to our restlessness. Remember, ambition is the root of restlessness. Whoever seeks peace has to let go of ambition. Peace begins where ambition ends.

Joshua Liebman has written, "As a young man full of exuberant fancy, I set down my inventory of earthly desirables to find fulfillment: health, love, beauty, talent, power, riches, and fame – together with several minor ingredients of what I considered man's perfect portion." He took that list to an elder and said to him, "If someone possesses all this, he would be like a god."

He notes, "At the corners of my friend's old eyes, I saw wrinkles of amusement gathering in a patient net. 'An excellent list,' he said, pondering it thoughtfully. 'But it appears, my young friend, that you have omitted the most important element of all. You have forgotten the one ingredient, lacking which each possession becomes a hideous torment, and your list as a whole an intolerable burden.'

"'And what,' I asked, 'is that missing ingredient?'

"With a pencil stub he crossed out my entire schedule. Then, having demolished my adolescent dream-structure at a single stroke, he wrote three syllables: peace of mind."

Seek peace. But remember that if you don't find it in yourself, then you won't be able to find it anywhere else.

Peace is not an external object. It is something you create yourself that connects you to your inner music, which is always there in every situation. Peace is the very word for someone's inner being becoming musical. It is not some vacant and empty state of mind, but a very positive state of the feeling of music.

Everything that is valuable in this world – life, love or beauty – has to be discovered yourself. There is no way you can get them from anyone else.

I am reminded of a very strange conversation:

During the First World War, two friends were talking in a trench full of dead, dying, and wounded soldiers. One of them was at death's door. He knew he was about to die, that he had only a short while to live. He told his friend, who was lying right next to him, "Listen, my friend. I know that your life has not been good. You have committed many crimes, made many unforgivable mistakes and their dark shadows have always followed you. You have experienced a lot of suffering and shame because of them. But the authorities don't have anything against my name. I have no blots on my record. So why don't you take my name, my identity number and my life. And let me take your name, your identity number and your life. As it is, I am about to die. Let me take all your crimes and dark deeds with me! Don't delay. Here, take my papers – and give me yours."

How sweet are these words uttered in love! But if only this were possible. Can a life ever be exchanged? Names and papers can be exchanged because they are not life. How can you exchange life with someone else? Neither can you live in anybody else's place, nor can you die in place of anyone else. Indeed, no one can ever be at exactly the same point as the being of anyone else. There is no way you can take on yourself the sins or good deeds of someone else. This is impossible. Life is not something which can be exchanged. It is something you have to create yourself, out of your own being.

The second soldier embraced his dying friend with all his heart and said, "Please forgive me. But even if I take your name and papers, I will still be the same person I am now. I may appear to be a different person to others, but the real question is to existence. Exchanged papers will not be able to deceive those eyes."

Everyone has to create their own life, just as a person learns to dance. It is not like painting pictures or making sculptures. In life, the creator and the creation are one and the same. So you cannot gift your life to anyone, nor can you borrow it from someone else. Life is nontransferable.

If we could only become peaceful, silencing all the words and sounds echoing inside, we could see what is fundamental in life. To see truth, we need the eyes of peace. He who searches for truth before finding those eyes searches in vain.

The Zen master Rinzai was one day giving a discourse. He said, "Inside each person, in everyone's body, lies hidden a being which has no adjectives, status or name. It is this title-less being that shines through the windows of the body. Those who have never seen this should do so now. They should see. See! Friends, look! Look!"

Hearing this, a monk stood up and asked, "Who is this being of truth? Who is this title-less entity?"

Rinzai climbed down from the pulpit and passed through the crowd of monks to reach the questioner. Everyone was astonished: instead of answering, what was he doing? He caught hold of the monk tightly and said, "Ask me again." The monk was afraid and didn't speak.

Rinzai said, "Look inside. That one there – peaceful and silent – that is the being of truth. That is you. Just recognize it. All the doors of truth will open up for you if you recognize it."

Look at a lake on a full-moon night. If the lake is calm, it reflects the moon. The mind is just like that. When there are no waves in it, it reflects truth. He whose mind is covered with waves keeps truth away. Truth is always nearby, but because of our own restlessness we are not always near it.

38 Life is a soap bubble. Those who don't see it like that are drowned and destroyed in it. But those who become aware of this truth start searching for a life which is eternal.

A mystic was once imprisoned. He had uttered a few truths which the emperor didn't like at all. A friend visited him in prison and asked, "Why did you unnecessarily get yourself into all this trouble? What harm would there have been if you hadn't said those things?"

The mystic said, "I can only speak the truth now. I cannot even think of saying anything false. Since I experienced a glimpse of godliness in my life, truth is my only option. And this imprisonment will only be for a short while."

Somebody went and told the emperor this. The emperor said, "Go and tell that mad mystic that his imprisonment is not for a short while, but for life."

When the mystic heard this, he laughed and said, "Please go and tell the dear emperor that the mad mystic has asked, 'Is life there for more than a short while?'"

Those who want to find real life will have to understand the truth about this so-called life of ours. And those who make an effort to understand its truth discover that its reality and its meaning are no more than a dream.

What do I teach? I teach only one thing: there is noth-ing worth following except your own inner being. He who discovers the light there, his whole life becomes full of light. Then he doesn't need the help of lamps on the outside, nor does he need to follow the smoky trail of other people's torches. Only when someone becomes free of the need for these, does he find the grandeur and greatness of the soul.

There was a very learned man who had studied a lot. He was an expert on all the Vedas and the scriptures and was full of ego about his intellectual achievements. He always walked with a burning torch in his hand; day or night, the torch was always with him. Whenever any-one asked him why, he would reply, "The world is in such darkness. I carry this torch so that people can at least have some light. Apart from this torch, what other light is there on their dark path of life?"

One day, a monk heard these words and started laughing. He said, "My friend, even if your eyes are blind to the sun, that universal giver of light, at least stop say-ing the world is filled with darkness. What more glory can your torch add to the already existing greatness of the sun? Do you think people who can't even see the sun will be able to see your measly torch?"

Buddha once told this story and I wished to tell it again. Now there are many torches flaring in the sky, not just one. All around, on every path, there are torches – of religions, of sects, of ideologies, of isms. And they all are claiming the same: that apart from them, there is no other light. They are all eager to light up your dark pathways. But the truth is that it is their smoky torches that prevent the eyes of man from seeing the sun. All these torches have to be extinguished so that man can see the sun. The only real light is the sun created by existence, not any man-made torch.

Turn your eyes in and see the sun which is inside you. There is no light apart from that light. Seek refuge only in that. He who seeks out any different refuge is simply insulting the godliness living inside.

What is bliss? Happiness is a kind of excitement and **40** so is unhappiness. The excitement that we like, we call happiness, and the one we don't like, we call unhappiness. Bliss is totally different from either. It is not a state of excitement, but of peace. He who wants happiness always falls into unhappiness – because after one excitement, the opposite excitement is as unavoidable as valleys with mountains, and nights with days. But he who is ready to let go of both happiness and unhappiness finds the bliss that is eternal.

Huang Po often told a story:

A man's only son had disappeared. He had been lost for twelve years and even the man himself was tired of searching for him. Slowly, slowly, he forgot about the whole thing.

After many years, a stranger came to his door and said, "I am your son. Don't you recognize me?" The father was very happy. He gave a big feast to welcome his son back home, inviting all his friends. There were great celebrations and festivities. But he had so totally forgotten his son that he did not recognize this claimant. After a few days, he did recognize him and saw that the man was not his son. At the first opportunity, the man ran off with all his wealth.

Huang Po used to say that such claimants come to everyone's house, but very few people are able to recognize them. Most are taken in by them and lose all their life's wealth.

Those who take bliss to be the pleasure they get from pleasant activities or objects, instead of the real bliss that arises from their being, will destroy the invaluable wealth of life with their own hands.

Always remember that whatever you get from outside will also be taken away. It is a mistake to think that it is yours. Only what arises from within your own being is yours. And that is the real wealth. Those who look for something else instead, no matter what they may get, ultimately find they have achieved nothing at all. On the contrary, they have wasted their whole life in a mad rat race.

If you want to find godliness, learn how to die. Don't you see that when the seed dies, it becomes a tree?

Someone had gone to see a Baul mystic. He was lost in singing a song; his eyes did not seem to be looking at this world and even his soul did not seem to be there. He was somewhere else – in some other world, in some other state.

When he stopped singing and seemed to be coming back, the visitor asked him, "How do you think *moksha*, ultimate liberation, can be attained?"

The mystic, who had an enchanting voice, replied, "Only through death."

I was telling this to someone yesterday. He asked me, "Through death?" and I said yes, by dying while you are still alive. Only he who dies to everything else becomes alive and awake to truth.

There is no greater art than learning how to die while you are still alive. This is the only art which I call yoga. A man who lives with an awareness of death certainly comes to know everything that is essential in life.

42 Don't waste your life just building earthly homes. And remember the immortal home you have left behind, that you will return to in the future. Once you remember that place, you will no longer consider those homes to be homes.

Some children were playing with sand on the bank of a river. They had made houses of sand and each was proclaiming, "This is my house. Mine is the best and nobody else can have it." They went on playing like this, and if one of them damaged another's house in some way, they quarreled, they fought. Slowly the darkness of dusk began to gather and they remembered that they had to go home. Just like that, they left their houses and palaces; none of them thought anymore about "mine" and "yours."

I read this parable somewhere and I thought how true this small story is. Aren't we all also like small children building castles in the sand? How few people are reminded about going home when they see the sun setting! And don't most people leave this world still carrying a sense of "mine" and "yours" about their houses of sand?

Remember, maturity has no relation whatsoever to age. I call someone mature who no longer has faith in earthly homes. The others are just children playing with sand castles.

The bliss of love and prayer lies within – not outside. **43**
And he who wants something else from love and prayer,
or through them, knows nothing of their secret. To be
drowned in love is the very fruit of love. And the bliss of
being absorbed in prayer is the very reward of prayer.

A religious devotee had been practicing spiritual dis-
ciplines for many years. One night, he had a dream in
which he heard someone say to him, "It is not in your destiny to find God, so don't unnecessarily waste your time
and effort." He told his friends about the dream, but the
dream didn't make him sad, nor did he stop praying.

His friends said to him, "When you have already been
told that the doors of destiny are sealed against you, why
are you still unnecessarily praying?"

The devotee replied, "Unnecessarily praying? You
fools! Praying is bliss in itself. What has it got to do with
getting or not getting anything? Besides, when someone who wants something has his desire thwarted at one
door, he can knock at another – but for me, where is the
second door? The door to God is the only door I have."
That night he saw that God was embracing him.

It is impossible not to find for those whose only longing is for God. Merging all desires into one gives man
power, making him capable of transcending himself and
entering the cosmic consciousness.

44

I sought many kinds of wealth, but I found them all, in the end, to be a loss. Then I searched for the wealth within myself. What I found was godliness. Then I realized that losing godliness is truly a loss, and finding it is the only wealth.

Somebody once praised an emperor with many words. He sang many beautiful songs to the emperor's glory, expecting to receive something in return. The emperor laughed at all the praises heaped on him, and then presented the man with a lot of gold coins. When he looked at the coins, the man's eyes filled with an extraordinary shine and he looked up toward the sky. Something was written on those coins. He threw them away and started dancing; his state had changed dramatically. An amazing inner revolution had happened from reading what was on the coins. After many years, somebody asked him what was written on the coins. He replied, "On the gold coins it said: 'God is enough.'"

Truly, God is enough. Those who know all agree with this truth.

What did I see? I saw that people who have everything are poor; I saw very wealthy people who actually have nothing. Then I stumbled upon this key – that those who want to attain everything have to let go of everything. Those who dare to let go of everything become worthy of godliness.

What is life? Enter the mystery of life. By merely living you can exhaust life, but you cannot know it. Use your energy not to merely live life, but also to know it. One who comes to know it is able to live it too.

45

Last night, some strangers came. They had some problems and I asked them about it. One of them asked, "What is death?" I was a little amazed because problems are about life. What problem can there be about death? Then I told them about a conversation between Confucius and Chi-Lu.

Chi-Lu asked Confucius before he died, "How should one honor and serve dead souls?"

Confucius said, "When you are unable to look after living people, how will you be able to look after dead souls?"

Then Chi-Lu asked, "Can I ask something about the nature of death?"

Confucius, who was very old and at death's door, replied, "When you don't even know about life yet, how can you know about death?"

This answer is very significant. Only those who come to know life can know death. For those who come to know the mystery of life, death too is no longer a mystery because it is merely the other side of the coin.

Only those who do not know life fear death. Someone whose fear of death has gone has met life. It is known only at someone's death whether they really knew life. Look inside yourself: if you find the fear of death lingering there, know that you have not yet known life.

46 When the inner state is calm and the vision harmonious, the feeling that arises then is the door to the ultimate reality. Those whose inner state is disturbed and whose vision is not harmonious are, in the same proportion, far from truth. Sri Aurobindo has said, "To be harmonious is to be infinite." To be disharmonious is to be tiny. And the moment you are in harmony, you gain the right to infinity.

Someone asked, "What is religion?" I said: a state of inner harmony. The person who had asked the question didn't seem to understand, so he asked again. I said to him that there is a state of consciousness where nothing troubles or disturbs. In that state, light and darkness seem the same, and happiness and unhappiness are equally welcomed and accepted. That is the religious state of consciousness. It is the state in which bliss is born; where even enemies do not oppose each other and where no choice is ever made. In this state, someone can enter within himself.

As he was about to leave, I remembered something. I said: Listen! There was a monk called Joshu. Somebody asked him, "Is there one single word which represents religion?"

Joshu said, "In the very asking it becomes two." But the questioner persisted, so Joshu said, "The word is yes."

To accept life in its entirety and totality is to reach the state of inner harmony. That is what *samadhi*, or no-mind, is. Only in that state does the "I" dissolve and union happen with the whole. He who has a no in his mind cannot become one with the whole. To experience a yes toward the whole is the greatest revolution in life, because it erases the ego and introduces us to our true self.

I have known the state of inner harmony to be the greatest wealth. Inner harmony is unparalleled and only when you find this state in yourself do you find bliss and immortality. It is a declaration that you yourself are the ultimate reality. Krishna's assurance is: inner harmony itself is the ultimate reality.

47 Remember that in this world nothing is attainable except your being. Those who search for it find it; those who search for anything else find only failure and anguish. People chasing after desires are always destroyed – they are being destroyed and will go on being destroyed. That is the path to self-destruction.

Once a small child, still crawling, noticed his shadow while playing in the sun. It seemed to be a marvelous thing because if he moved, his shadow moved with him. He started trying to catch the shadow's head, but whenever he lurched forward to catch it, it had moved away. No matter how much he reached for it, he found that the head always eluded him by the same distance. The distance between him and the shadow never shrank, so he cried from weariness and failure.

A passing monk, who had come to beg for alms and was standing at the door, saw all this. He stepped forward and put the child's hand on his own head. The child who had been crying, now started laughing. This way he had managed to catch the shadow's head!

Yesterday I told this story and said: it is essential that you place your hand on your being. Those who try to catch hold of the shadow are never able to do so. The body is the shadow. If you keep trying, you will definitely weep one day.

Desires are insatiable. No matter how much you chase after them, they will always remain unfulfilled. Freedom from them comes only when someone turns back to himself and settles in his own being.

A man who has no endurance soon falls apart. But someone who wears the shield of endurance finds that life's constant battering only makes him stronger.

I have heard...

A man was passing a blacksmith's shop. He heard the sound of a hammer constantly banging on the anvil, so he peered inside the shop. He saw many broken and twisted hammers lying in a corner; only time and use could have done that to them. The man asked the blacksmith, "How many anvils did you need to reduce those hammers to such a state?"

The blacksmith started laughing and said, "Only one, my friend. A single anvil breaks hundreds of hammers because the hammers strike and the anvil endures."

It is true that the man who wins in the end is the one who accepts all life's poundings with patience. He too hears a lot of banging in his life, just like the noise of a hammer falling on the anvil, but eventually the hammer breaks and the anvil remains, safe and sound.

49

You want bliss? You want light? Then first search within your self. He who searches there does not have to search anywhere else. And he who doesn't search there keeps searching without ever finding.

There was once a beggar. He begged his whole life sitting in one particular place. He had a strong desire to be rich and he begged for a long time. But has anyone ever become rich through begging? He was a beggar and remained a beggar. He lived a beggar and died a beggar. When he died, he did not even have enough money for his last rites. After his death, people tore down his hut and cleared out the place where he used to sit; a huge treasure was found buried right under the spot where he had sat and begged all his life!

I would like to ask everyone: Aren't we too all like that beggar? Isn't that treasure, which we spend our whole life searching for outside, hidden inside each of us?

Before starting your journey in search of peace and treasure, first dig where you are standing. The greatest treasure seekers and explorers, after wandering endlessly all over the world, have found the treasure right there.

Religion is one. Truth is one. And those who see it divided should understand that it is their own eyes which are divided.

There once was a goldsmith who was a devotee of Rama. He had such a blind devotion that he had no respect for any statue other than that of Rama. He would never even look at another statue. In fact, he used to close his eyes in front of other statues!

One day, the emperor of the country ordered him to make a crown studded with gems for a statue of Krishna. The goldsmith found himself in a great dilemma: how could he measure the head of Krishna's statue? Somehow, with his eyes blindfolded, he started to take the measurements. But as he was doing it, he had the same feeling as if he was touching the familiar statue of his own beloved Rama! He was so astonished at this that, in one swift move, he threw the blindfold from his eyes. In that instant, not only was his outer blindfold thrown away, but also the inner one. For the first time, his eyes were really open and he could see that every form is a manifestation of God because he has no form of his own. No other form can belong to something which has a form of its own. Only something that has no form can contain all forms.

Whether this story is true or not, I do not know. But every day I see similar blindfolds over the eyes of people going to temples, mosques and churches. I tell them this story. When they ask me if it is true, I tell them: if you look for the blindfold over your own eyes, you will see that at least half the story is true. And if you then throw away the outer blindfold, the other half of the story would also become true!

Open your eyes and see. With our own hands we are depriving ourselves of the wholeness of truth. He who sees, dropping all concepts and prejudices, experiences only one reality, one God, present everywhere.

51

What is self-discipline? When you are unaffected by the feeling of touch, that is self-discipline. A neutral sense of witnessing is self-discipline. "To be" in the world and at the same time "not to be" in the world, is self-discipline.

Once Yen-Hui asked Confucius, "What should I do to have mental self-discipline?"

Confucius said, "You never listen just with your ears, you listen with your mind. In fact, not even with the mind, you identify yourself totally with what you hear. Try listening just with your ears. There is no need for the mind to help the ears. In that state of nothingness, your soul will receive impressions from the outside in just a passive way. Self-discipline lies in such a state of *samadhi* or no-mind. And godliness too lives only in such a state."

Yen-Hui said, "But in this way my personality will be lost! Is this what the state of nothingness means?"

Confucius said, "Yes, that is the meaning. Do you see that window in front of you? Its presence makes it possible for this room to be lit with the beauty of the natural scenery. But the scenery is totally outside. If you want to, you can use your eyes and ears in a similar way to light your inside. Let the senses be your windows and become empty. This is the state I call self-discipline."

I see with my eyes, listen with my ears, walk with my feet – but still I am distant from them all; where I am, there is no seeing, no listening, no walking. Learn to stand apart, neutral and untouched by whatever comes through the senses. To be settled like that, in the state of being untouched, is self-discipline. And self-discipline is the door to truth.

Light has no idea of darkness. Light only knows light. Those whose hearts have become pure and full of light cannot see impurity or darkness in any other heart. As long as we see impurity, we can be sure that some remnants of impurity remain in us. It is simply an indication that we are impure.

The notes of the morning prayer were echoing in the temple.

Acharya Ramanuja was walking around the temple, immersed in prayers for God, when suddenly an untouchable woman came in his way. Seeing her, he was upset, his so-called absorption in prayer was disturbed and harsh words came from his mouth: "You, untouchable woman, get out of my way and don't defile my path." There was anger in the eyes that had been in prayer a moment before, and venom on the lips that had been singing praises of the lord.

But the woman did not move. Instead, with folded hands, she asked, "Master, where should I move to? God's purity is all around, everywhere! So in which direction should I take my impurity?"

Ramanuja looked at the woman as if a veil had been lifted from his eyes. Those few words of hers swept away all the harshness from his face. Bowing in reverence he said, "Mother, forgive me. It is our own inner dirt that we see outside. Someone who wears the kohl of inner purity in his eyes sees only sacredness all around."

I know of no other path to see God. There is only one path and that is to experience the divine all around.

Someone who begins to see God in everything, he – and only he – can have the key to God's door.

A young man asked me, "What is worth saving in life?" **53**
I said: your own soul and its music. He who is able to save
that has saved everything; and he who loses that loses
everything.

An elderly musician, passing through a forest carrying many gold coins, was captured by thieves. As well as
stealing all his money, they also took his violin. Nobody
could equal that musician on the violin; nobody had a
greater claim to that instrument. The old man asked very
politely for his violin back. The thieves were amazed –
why was the old man asking for the return of an ordinary
violin of little value, rather than demanding his money
back? They realized that a violin was of no use to them,
so they returned it to him. Receiving it, the musician
started dancing with joy, and he sat down right there and
began to play.

It was a dark, no-moon night. A lonely forest. The
echoing notes of his violin seemed otherworldly in the
stillness of that dark forest. At first the thieves listened
without much interest, but slowly their eyes softened and
grew misty, and they began to sway with the melody of
the music. Eventually they were so overwhelmed by his
music that they fell at his feet and begged forgiveness.
They not only returned all his wealth, but also gave him
a lot more money as a gift and safely escorted him out
of the forest.

Isn't every human being in the same situation? Isn't
every man robbed every day? But how many would think
of saving their music and the instrument of that music,
rather than saving their wealth?

Leave everything else and save your music, and the instrument that gives birth to the music of life. Those who have even a little understanding do just that. And those who fail to do so, even if they acquire all the wealth in the world, it has no value. Remember that man has no greater wealth than his own inner music.

54

When I see someone dying, I experience that I too have died in his death. Certainly, each death brings news of my own death. And those who cannot see this seem blind to me. I have learned from each and every happening in this world. And the more I looked deeper into them, the more non-attachment spontaneously happened. If our eyes are open in the world, it brings wisdom. And when wisdom comes, non-attachment follows.

I have heard that a very old beggar used to sit by the roadside and beg. His body was paralyzed, he was blind and his whole body bore the effects of leprosy. People would look the other way when they passed him. A young man who used to pass that way every day wondered how such a tattered, worn out, half-dead old man could have such a lust for life. Why did he want to live, even as a beggar?

Finally, one day he asked the old man that question. Hearing it, the beggar laughed and said, "Son! The same question troubles my mind also. And when I ask God, I don't get any answer there either. So I think perhaps God wants me to continue living so that others can see me and realize that once I was like them, and that they too can become like me one day! In this world, the ego of beauty, health and youth is just a deception."

The body is a constantly changing flow, and so is the mind. Those who take them to be the shore, drown. The body is not the shore, nor is the mind. The only true shore is the consciousness, the witness, the watcher which lies behind them both – that unchanging, eternal, awareness. Those who tie their boats to that shore attain the immortal.

Desires make man a pauper. It is desires that give birth to bondage and begging and there is no end to them, either. The more they are shed, the richer and more independent someone becomes. For the man who desires nothing, his freedom is endless.

A sannyasin had some money and announced that he wanted to give it to the poor. Many poor people surrounded him and began begging for the money. He said, "I will give it immediately. I will give it to the most hungry and destitute person in the world!" Saying that, he went inside his house.

Suddenly people saw that the king's entourage was passing and became absorbed in watching the procession. In the meanwhile the sannyasin came out and, seeing the king sitting on his elephant, threw the money to him.

The king was astonished and asked him to explain his actions. The people also accosted the sann-yasin, saying, "You said you would give the money only to the most destitute person!"

The sannyasin laughed and replied, "Yes, I have given it to the most destitute person. Isn't the most destitute person the one who surpasses everyone else in his hunger for wealth?"

What is unhappiness? Unhappiness is a desire to get something and to become something. No one wants unhappiness, but as long as you have desires, you will have unhappiness. He who has understood the nature of desire does not seek freedom from unhappiness, but from desires themselves. And then the door to unhappiness closes automatically.

People who cannot make anything of their life often become critics. People who cannot walk life's path usually stand by the side of the road and throw stones at others. This is a very sick state of mind. Whenever the feeling arises in your mind to condemn someone, be aware that you are in the grip of the same disease. A healthy person never condemns anyone. And when others condemn him, he just feels sorry for them. Not only the physically sick, but also the mentally sick deserve pity.

Norman Vincent Peale has written somewhere, "I have a friend who is a well-known social worker. He is often heavily slandered and criticized, but nobody has ever seen him lose his cool. When I asked him the secret, he said, 'Kindly show me one of your fingers.' Surprised, I showed him one of my fingers. He started laughing and said, 'Do you see! One of your fingers is pointing at me, but the remaining three are pointing at you. Actually, whenever anyone raises a finger at someone else, without being aware of it, three fingers start pointing back at him. So when anyone takes a bad shot at me, my heart feels pity for him because he is hurting himself much more than he could ever hurt me."

Whenever someone criticizes you, always remember this immortal saying of Aristotle. Hearing that some people had declared him to be a very bad man, he said, "I will always try to live in such a way that no one will ever believe what they are saying."

57 Find love. There is nothing higher than that. Tiruvalluvar has said, "Love is the very soul of life. He who has no love in him is merely a heap of bones covered with flesh."

Someone asked me yesterday, "What is love?" I said: whatever love may be, there is no way of putting it into words because it is not a thought. Love is an experience. You can be drowned in it, but you cannot know it. Don't think about love. Stop thinking and see the world. What you will experience then, in that peaceful state, is love.

And then I told a story:

A pundit once asked a Baul mystic, "Do you know all the forms of love, as they are described in the scriptures?"

The Baul replied, "How can an ignorant person like me know what is written in the scriptures?" Hearing this, the pundit described to the Baul in detail all the categories of love mentioned in the scriptures, and then asked him what he thought about them.

The mystic started laughing and said, "Hearing you talk, I was beginning to feel as if a goldsmith had entered a garden and was rubbing and testing the beauty of the flowers on the touchstone he uses for testing gold!"

Don't think about love – live it. But remember that in living it, you will have to lose your self. Ego is the opposite to love; the more you lose your ego, the more you will be filled with love. When the ego is zero, love is all. It is this love which is the ladder to the door of God.

Flowers come and go. Thorns come and go. Happiness comes and goes. Unhappiness comes and goes. The life of he who comes to know this eternal law of change in the universe will be free of all limitations.

One dark night, a man standing on the bank of a river was contemplating suicide by jumping in. It was rainy season and the river was in full flow. The sky was full of dark clouds and every now and then lightning flashed. The man had been one of the wealthiest in the country, but through sudden losses all his wealth was gone. The sun seemed to have set on his luck and he could see nothing but darkness ahead, so he had made up his mind to put an end to himself. But as he was about to reach the edge of the rock to jump into the river, a pair of old but strong hands held him.

Just then, there was a flash of lightning and he saw that it was an old sannyasin holding him.

The old man asked him why he was in despair and, hearing the story, he started laughing and said, "So you agree that before all this happened you were happy?"

The man said, "Yes, certainly. The sun was shining high on my luck and now only darkness is left in my life."

The old man started laughing again and said, "Day follows night and night follows day. When the day doesn't last, how can the night? Change is the law of nature. Listen carefully: if the good days didn't last, the bad days also won't last. And he who understands this truth is neither elated with happiness nor depressed with unhappiness. His life becomes like an immovable rock which remains the same in rain or sun."

He who accepts both unhappiness and happiness with serenity has found his soul – because it is the awareness of being separate from both that brings serenity. Happiness and unhappiness come and go. That which neither comes nor goes is man's isness, and to be at rest with that isness is serenity.

59

To forget the "I," to rise above the "I," is the greatest art. It is only by transcending it that man crosses the threshold from being a person to connecting with godliness. Those who remain enclosed in their "I" cannot experience godliness. Other than this confinement, there is no obstacle between man and godliness.

Chuang Tzu used to tell a story of a carpenter:

This carpenter was a genius in his work. The things he made were so beautiful that people would often praise him by saying it was as if they were made by the gods, not a human. A king once asked him, "What is this magic in your art?"

The carpenter replied, "Your Majesty, there is no magic involved at all! It is a very small thing: whatever I make, while making it, I put my "I" aside. First of all, I stop wasting my life energy and make my mind utterly peaceful. After living this way for three days, I completely forget about the profit and the financial side of the product. After five days, I even forget about the fame that this object will bring me. Seven days, and I even become oblivious to my body. This way my whole skill becomes focused – all inner and outer obstacles and choices vanish. Then nothing remains except what I am creating. Even I do not exist. That is why those creations seem godly."

This is the secret formula to bring godliness into your life. Forget the "I" and let your consciousness be absorbed in some creation. Disappear in your creation and become one with it, the way existence has become one with its creation.

Yesterday somebody asked me, "What should I do?" I said: what you do is not as important as how you do it. Do something from the space of having dropped yourself, your "I," and in that doing, you will find the way to the self.

Some people had come this morning and I told them: always try to go deeper and deeper into yourself. There should be such a depth inside that it is immeasurable. He who goes deep beyond measure reaches unbelievable heights. The heights of life are directly related to the depths. Those who want height, but not depth, will certainly fail. The peaks of height are supported by the depth – there is no other way. The real thing is the depth; those who find it will automatically reach the heights. Only those who have depth inside, like an ocean, can reach the heights of the snow-peaked mountains. Depth is the price which must be paid to reach the heights. And remember, nothing in life is ever free.

Ramateertha used to say that in Japan he had seen pine and cedar trees which were three to four hundred years old, but less than a foot high. You must have seen how great and tall pine and cedar trees grow. Then who stops those trees from growing, and how? When he inquired about it, he was told that they don't touch the leaves and branches, but they keep cutting the roots to prevent them from growing downward. And the rule is that unless roots grow downward, a tree will not grow upward.

There is a relationship between above and below, so those who want to attain to the heights must spread roots deep into the soul. If the roots do not grow inward, then life can never rise upward. But we have totally forgotten this rule and, as a result, lives which could have risen high like cedars can't rise even a foot above their base. Man becomes smaller and smaller because the roots into his soul become shallower and shallower.

The body is the surface, the soul is the depth. How can he who lives only in the body find depth? Live in the soul, not in the body. Always remember that whatever you think, speak or do, should not be limited to the body. Think, speak and act also on a level higher than the body. Only through that, do roots gradually grow into the soul and reach the depth.

Be as you would like others to be. To change others, first you have to change yourself. Only if you transform yourself, can you trigger the transformation of others.

Only he who is fully awake can be of any help to others. How can someone who is asleep wake others up? And how can someone in darkness become a source of light to others? He can help others only when he has realized his own self – that is certain. Caring for the well-being of others is impossible if you haven't first taken care of your own well-being.

Someone was telling me, "I would like to serve others." and I told him: first spiritual discipline, then service. How can you give others something when you don't even have it yourself? First find it through spiritual discipline, only then can you share through helping others.

Many people want to help others, but no one wants to make their own spiritual discipline and realize their own self. It is like wanting to reap a harvest without having sown any seed! It is not possible.

A very poor, weak man asked Buddha, "My Lord, what shall I do to help mankind?" The man was not weak in the body, but in the soul; he was not poor in wealth, but in life.

Buddha looked at him for a moment with profound compassion. His eyes moistened with pity. He made just a small statement, but how much compassion and meaning it carried! He asked, "What will you be able to do?" Repeat this in your own minds: "What will you be able to do?" All doing begins with the self and arises from the self. He who wants to do something for others, without first having done it for himself is sadly mistaken. Realizing the self, becoming healthy, just that is service.

Service is not done. It flows spontaneously from love. And love? Love is nothing but the overflowing of bliss. What is bliss inside becomes love in action.

The heights and depths that any human being has ever reached can be reached by anyone else, at any time. And man will even reach heights and depths which nobody has yet reached; remember, the power of man is infinite.

I can see infinite energy lying dormant in every human being. But most of this energy remains still asleep and locked up as the hour of death arrives. We do not energize and activate this energy and potential, so most of us live only half alive, and some even less than that. We use only a part of our physical and mental energies, and never use our spiritual energy at all. We tap into only the minimum of sources of energy hidden in us, and this is the fundamental cause of our inner poverty.

William James has said that man's fire burns dim, and that's why even in front of his own soul he feels immensely inferior. It is absolutely essential to rise above this inferiority. There is no greater sin than to remain helpless and wretched through our own choice. If you dig the earth, hidden springs of water are found; similarly, those who learn to dig into their own being find infinite sources of energy hidden inside. But for that, he has to become active and creative.

He who wants to find his whole being takes positive action – while others just go on thinking about it. He who knows a little, converts it immediately into action; he doesn't wait to know a lot. That way, spade by spade, he digs the well of energy inside him, while people who just think, remain sitting. It is only through positive action and creativity that dormant energies wake up and man becomes more and more alive. The man who activates all his potential energy can experience life in its totality, and he alone will experience his being as well. The experience that happens when man realizes his full potential *is* the being.

Don't stop at thinking. Move and do something. It is more valuable to take even a single step than to just think about walking a thousand miles, because that one step at least takes you somewhere.

Is there any power greater than love? No. Because when you find love, you become free of fear.

A young man was on a sea cruise with his newly-wed bride. As the sun set and the deep dark of night descended, suddenly there was a fierce storm. All the passengers were very afraid; their lives were at stake and the ship felt as if it could sink any moment. But the young man didn't seem to be worried at all. His wife shakily asked, "How come you are sitting there, so carefree? Don't you see that with every passing moment the chances of our survival become slimmer and slimmer?"

The young man pulled his sword from its sheath and, putting it to his wife's neck, asked, "Are you afraid? Is your life in danger now from my sword?"

His wife started laughing and replied, "What is this idiocy? I have no reason to feel scared of a sword that is in your hands!"

The young man said, "Ever since I had a glimpse of existence, I have the same feeling toward it." When there is love, fear simply does not exist.

Love is fearlessness. The absence of love is fear. Someone who wants to transcend fear will have to become full of love for the whole of existence. From one door of consciousness, love enters; from the other, fear exits.

64 Life follows either desires, or awareness. Desires promise contentment, but they actually make you more discontent. That is why the eyes must be closed to follow desire. He who opens his eyes and looks, attains awareness. And in the fire of awareness, all discontent evaporates like dew-drops in the sun.

A biologist called Doctor Fabre talks about an insect, a kind of caterpillar, which always follows its leader. He took a group of them and put them on a round plate. Once they started walking they kept on walking – they kept going round and round in a circle. Since the path was circular, it had no end. But they didn't seem to real-ize this, and kept walking till they dropped dead from exhaustion. Only death could stop their walking. They never realized that the path they were walking was actu-ally not a path, but a circle.

A path leads you somewhere; a circle never gets you anywhere – it just makes you go round and round. When I look around, I find this is exactly the situation of man. He also keeps walking, and never seem to stop and think whether the path he is on is a circular rut! The path of desire is circular. We keep coming back again and again to the same desires. That is why desires are insatia-ble; no one can ever get anywhere by following them. Contentment is impossible on that path. But there are a few blessed people who are able to wake up from this useless, ignorant journey before death overtakes them.

When I see people treading the path of desires, my heart weeps for them because they are on a path that will never take them anywhere. In the end, they will find that they have wasted their whole life chasing dreams. Mohammed has said, "Who can be more lost than the man who is chasing desires?"

65 Someone asked, "What do you think about ambition?" I said: there are very few people who are really ambitious. People who are easily satisfied with the trivial cannot really be called ambitious. Only people who aspire to the infinite are truly ambitious. We generally consider ambition to be a bad thing. I say, no; real ambition is not bad at all, because it is that ambition which leads you toward godliness.

Many days ago, I had said to a young man: have an aim in life, and give your heart an ambition. Fill yourself with exalted dreams. Without an aim, you will not be able to become a complete person; without it, you will not be unified and your energies will remain scattered. Only he who can focus all his different energies and direct them toward a single purpose can become a healthy individual. Everyone else is like a chaotic crowd. Their inner voices all contradict each other and no melody ever arises in their life.

He who is not a melody unto himself can never find peace and strength. Peace and strength are two names of the same truth.

He asked how to do this and I said: look at a seed buried in the earth. See how it focuses all its energy and then breaks through the earth! Its thirst for the sun is what makes it sprout and grow. It is only because of that strong desire that it can break out of its shell and rise above the trivial. Be like that. Become like a seed. Be thirsty for the infinite, and then, focusing your energy, move upward. Then a moment comes when you are able to break out of yourself and find your real being.

He who keeps remembering the ultimate aim of life, his self, and truth, will not be content with anything else. This discontent is a blessing because it is only by passing through it that he can find the land of ultimate contentment.

66 Look how fleeting are the so-called pleasures of life. If you can see that, you will be free of them.

Someone narrated a folk tale:

A bird was floating in the sky. Right above her, shining in the distance, was a white cloud. She said to herself, "I would like to fly and touch that white cloud!" With this thought, and making that cloud her target, the bird flew with all her might in its direction. But the cloud sometimes suddenly moved east and sometimes west. Sometimes it would suddenly stop and start moving in circles. Then it started spreading. The bird had not even reached the cloud when it suddenly disintegrated and disappeared completely. With untiring tenacious effort, the bird reached the place where the cloud had been, only to find there was nothing there. Seeing this, the bird said to herself, "I was mistaken. I shouldn't make temporary clouds my target, but rather the proud mountains that are eternal and endless."

How true is this story! And how many of us don't fall victim to this mistake of making temporary clouds the goal of life? But look! Just nearby are also the eternal and endless mountains – making them the goal of life, we will find fulfillment and bliss.

Rabindranath has said somewhere: "A raindrop whispered in the ears of a jasmine flower, 'Beloved, keep me in your heart forever.' And before the jasmine could say anything, the raindrop fell to the ground."

Last night, an old man came to see me. His heart was full of complaints and complaints about life. I said to him: it is true that there are thorns on the path of life, but they are only seen by people who can't see the flowers. If you know how to see the flowers, then even thorns become flowers.

Farid uDin Attar often used to tell people, "O People of God, if anything bitter ever happens in life, then please remember that dear slave."

They would ask, "Which slave?" Then he would tell the following story:

A king once gave his slave a very rare and beautiful fruit. On tasting it, the slave remarked that the fruit was very sweet and that he had never seen or tasted such a fruit in his life. Hearing this, the king's mouth started watering. He told the slave to cut him a piece. But he saw that the slave was hesitant to part with even one piece, and his desire for it grew even more. Finally the slave had to give him a piece, but the moment the king put the fruit in his mouth, he discovered that it was very, very bitter. He looked at his slave in amazement!

The slave answered, "My Lord, you have given me many expensive gifts. Is their sweetness not sufficient to wipe out the bitterness of this little fruit? Should I complain about such a small thing and be unhappy? As it is, you have showered so many blessings on me, and for me to even think about this small bitterness would be showing ingratitude!"

The taste of life to a great extent depends on the way

we look at it. If someone wants he can see a small day between two dark nights. Or if he wants, he can see a small night between two days full of light. The first way makes even the day seem gloomy, while in the second, even the night is not a night.

What is a life without ideals? It is like a boat without a boatman, or if there is one, he is asleep. And you must always remember that there are many storms in the ocean of life. So without ideals the boat of your life will sink – it cannot help it.

Schweitzer has said, "The power of ideals cannot be measured. We do not see power in a drop of water. But let the same drop become ice in the crevice of a rock, and it will break the rock. Just a small change does something to the drop which makes it able to activate its hidden powers with such terrific results. Exactly the same applies to ideals. As long as they remain only as thoughts, their power has no effect. But when they solidify in someone's personality and behavior, then they produce tremendous power and great results."

Ideals are the desire to move from darkness to light. Someone not possessed by this desire goes on living in darkness. But ideals are not merely desires, they also carry a resolve – because a longing on its own, without a strong determination to back it up, doesn't mean anything at all. And an ideal is not just determination either, there is also a lot of ongoing effort involved.

No seed can ever become a tree without continuous effort.

I have heard, "An ideal which is not also backed up by a behavioral effort is useless. And a behavior which is not inspired by an ideal is very dangerous."

69 Man's mind is everything; it wants to know everything. But true knowing is found only by those who come to understand the mind itself.

Somebody was asking, "What should I do to find truth?" I said: enter your own being. And this can only be done by catching the mind by its roots. To worry about its branches and leaves is futile. To catch the mind by its roots, close your eyes and silently observe the thoughts. Start with any thought and watch it from its birth to its death.

Lu Kwan Wu has said: "Catch the thoughts just like a cat waiting for a mouse pounces on it." He is absolutely right. You must wait like a cat – eagerly, intensely and vigilantly. There should be no unaware lapse, even for a moment. When a thought arises, you must pounce on it and catch it. Then examine it properly. Observe – where was it born and where does it end? And as you go on observing, you will suddenly find that it has disappeared like a bubble in water, or vanished like a dream. You should do this with every thought that arises in you.

This practice greatly weakens the arrival of thoughts, and if you attack them continuously in this way, they will simply stop coming. When there are no thoughts, the mind becomes completely peaceful. And where the mind is peaceful, that is where its root is. He who catches hold of this root enters his own being. And to have entered the being, is to have found truth.

Truth is hidden in the knower itself. It is not discovered by knowing anything else. Only he who knows the knower itself attains truth. Do not run after the object of knowing. If you want to know, then you must chase the knower.

70

In the quest for truth, you will have to transform yourself. In fact, it is less of a search and more of a self-transformation. Those who are totally ready for this change, truth itself will come looking for them.

I have heard that the mystic Ibrahim used to relate this event from his life:

Before he became a sannyasin, he was the King of Balkh. One night, around midnight, he heard someone walking on the roof of his palace bedroom. He was very surprised and shouted, "Who is there?"

A reply came, "It is not an enemy."

He asked again, "But what are you doing up there?"

The reply was, "I am searching for my lost camel."

Ibrahim was amazed by these words, but he also couldn't help laughing at their foolishness. He said, "A camel lost on the roof of a tall palace is strange! Friend, are you in your right mind?"

In response, the stranger also started laughing and said, "You naïve one, isn't the state of mind in which you are searching for godliness even stranger than searching for a camel on the roof of a tall palace?"

Every day I get the opportunity to meet the type of people who want to find godliness without changing themselves. This is absolutely impossible – it cannot happen. Godliness is not some outer reality. It is nothing but the final refined state of our own consciousness. And to find it means simply becoming it ourselves.

I had been to a village and there someone asked me, **71** "What do you teach?" I said: I teach dreams. A man who doesn't dream about the other shore will never be able to launch his boat from this shore. It is dreams which give the courage to embark on the seemingly endless ocean.

A few young men had also come. I told them: don't just think about a livelihood, think also of a life. The eternal also exists, not just the temporal. And he who doesn't see that, just wastes his life in non-essentials.

They started saying, "Where is the time for such things? And anyway, doesn't all this talk of truth and eternity seem to be just a dream?" I listened to them and then said: friends, it is today's dreams that become tomorrow's truth. Don't be afraid of dreams, and never undermine them by calling them mere dreams, because there is no truth that was not originally born as a dream Truth is always born in the form of a dream. And blessed are those who live in the valleys, but are able to dream of the peaks; it is those very dreams which will stimulate them with longing and fill them with strength and determination to reach the heights. Think about it. In some solitary moment, pause and reflect over it. And also try to see that only today is in our hands – we have the right only to this moment. Understand that each moment of life is pregnant with many possibilities and it will never return again. To say that you don't have any time for dreams is very self-destructive. You needlessly tie your feet with your own hands. Such feelings will constrain and limit your mind within a certain boundary, and you will lose the wonderful freedom which is intrinsic to dreaming.

And also think of this – a huge amount of your time is spent on ventures which are completely useless, which can never come to fruition. How much time are you wasting in fighting over trivia, promoting arguments that come from your ego, slandering and criticizing? There are many such ways to waste time and energy. This valuable time can be transformed into learning about life, into self-reflection, self-examination and meditation. It is from this that the flowers whose fragrance is ethereal, and the music which is not of this world, are born.

Observe your dreams and analyze them because the vision of what you will be, and become tomorrow, is definitely hidden in them.

Ego is the only complexity. Those who wish to be simple will have to experience this truth. Experiencing this, simplicity will come as naturally as the shadow that follows you.

A sannyasin was visiting. When he came to see me, he said he had reduced all his needs to a bare minimum, and was still busy cutting them even further. When he said this, I saw in his eyes the same sense of achievement – a feeling of achieving something, a feeling of being something – that I had seen a few days earlier in the eyes of a young man who had just got a high position. It is the same feeling that a greedy man has when he gets money.

Any form of desire at the prospect of some fulfillment puts that glow in the eyes. It is the glow of the ego. And remember, to have a simple life, it is not enough to merely cut down on outer needs. The basis of a simple life is laid only when the ego is cut down inside. In fact, the needs automatically become simple as the ego lessens.

He who does the opposite, even though he may reduce his needs, will increase his ego; inner complexity, not simplicity, will be the result. You cannot get rid of complexity that way, it will only take on a new form and appearance. The ego is satisfied by the race to achieve something. Its life juice is "more and more." People who are busy collecting things are afflicted by this "more and more" mania, but people who renounce things are in the same bondage. In the end, both arrive at suffering and anguish because the ego is always empty. There is no way it can be filled. Only those who understand this truth and totally stop filling the ego can find true simplicity and non-possessiveness.

It is dangerous to discipline yourself to be non-possessive of outer things.

When there is no ego inside, possessiveness cannot survive on the outside. But never fall victim to the fallacy that if there are no possessions on the outside, the ego inside will disappear.

Possessiveness is not the root cause of ego, ego is the root cause of possessiveness.

73

Sow a few seeds of truth, goodness and beauty in life. Don't question what the seeds can achieve just because they are few. Hidden in each seed are thousands of seeds.

Always remember that a single seed can give birth to a whole garden.

Today I said to somebody: by spending very little time, I have experienced much. I devoted only a few moments to liberate the mind and have experienced phenomenal freedom. I spent just a few moments experiencing the beauty of flowers, waterfalls, the moon and the stars, and not only did I experience beauty, I found myself also becoming beautiful. I gave but a few moments to goodness, and it is difficult for me to describe the bliss I found. Since then, I have started saying it is very simple to experience godliness.

But if we are not ready to take even a few steps toward it, then that is very unfortunate. Give a little of your energy and time for truth, for peace, for beauty, for goodness – and you will see life's peaks coming closer and closer. A completely new world will open its doors, in whose womb many spiritual powers are hidden. He who longs for truth and peace will gradually find they are becoming his. And he who is inspired toward beauty and goodness will find them growing in himself.

As you get up in the morning, have a longing that today may bear some fruit toward truth, goodness and beauty. And check in the night whether you are closer to the peaks of life than yesterday. Self-observation gives birth to a deep longing for transformation and a deep longing transforms you.

He who wants to find truth needs to check each and **74**
every moment whether what he is doing will be a hindrance on the path to truth.

There is a story:
In a circus, there is an old artist who makes his wife
stand in front of a wooden board and then throws knives
at her. Each throw of the knife grazes and barely misses
different parts of her body – her throat, shoulders, arms
and legs – before sinking into the wood. Half an inch
wrong, and she would die.

He has been doing this show for thirty years. He has
also become utterly bored with his wife and fed up with
her quarreling and vicious nature; he has slowly built up
a huge hatred against her in his heart. One day, his mind
is so utterly poisoned by her behavior that he throws
the knife intending to kill her. He takes aim very carefully – he aims straight for the heart so everything will
be over in a flash. Then he throws the knife with his full
strength. Full of anger and excitement, he closes his
eyes. Mentally he visualizes the knife piercing her heart,
a fountain of blood gushing out and his wife dropping
dead with a heavy sigh.

Fearfully, he slowly opens his eyes, only to find his
wife standing there very much alive and smiling. The
knife had shot straight into the board as usual, missing
her body! He throws the other knives the same way – full
of anger, hatred and revenge, intended to kill – but each
time the knives hit the wood, as always. He looks at his
hands, tears of failure in his eyes, and he wonders what
has happened to his hands. He is not aware that he has

become so skilled and practiced that he is now a victim of his own art!

Similarly, we too have become so skilled in the false, in the bad, that creating the good and the beautiful becomes very difficult, even when we want to. Each day, and with our own hands, we go on restricting ourselves more and more. And the more we are restricted, the further we are from truth.

Each of our feelings, thoughts and actions create us. We are only the sum total of them. That is why he who wants to touch the peaks of truth will have to take care that he is not weighing himself down with stones instead of taking himself upward.

The path of life is filled with darkness. But remember, someone else's light is of no use in this darkness. Only your own light can be your companion. Those who put their faith in someone else's light just deceive themselves.

I have heard...

A master told his disciple, "Find the true knowledge. Except for that, there is no other way."

The disciple said, "I am dedicated to self-discipline. Is there still a need for knowledge if you discipline your behavior?"

The master replied, "My beloved! Have you ever seen the behavior of an elephant? He bathes in a lake and as soon as he comes out of the lake, he spreads dust all over his body. An ignorant person does exactly the same thing. In the absence of true knowing, discipline cannot keep your behavior pure for long."

The disciple very politely said, "Blessed one, a sick person just goes to the doctor, he doesn't try to study and have knowledge of medical science himself. You are my beacon light. I know one thing for sure, that you will never let me go on an irreligious path. So why do I need to find true knowledge?"

Hearing this, the master became very serious and told the following story: "There was an old brahmin. When he became blind, his children wanted him to have surgery on his eyes, but he refused. He said, 'Why do I need eyes? I have eight sons, eight daughters-in-law, and also your mother. Thirty-four eyes are available to me, so what difference does it make if there are two less?'

The father ignored the advice of his sons. Then one night, the house suddenly caught fire. Everyone ran out of the house to save their lives. No one remembered the old man and he was reduced to ashes in the fire.

That is why I say, my son, do not insist on ignorance. Knowing means having your own eyes. There is no other security than that."

Truth cannot be had from scriptures, nor from people who are the source of the scriptures. The door to find it is inside yourself. Only those who look inside themselves find it. Faith in his own self is the only strength for help-less man.

Find a single ray of truth, and that ray will radically transform you. Those who can have even a glimpse of it will inevitably experience a great revolution.

Gustav Meyrink wrote in a memoir that a Chinese friend once sent him a very beautiful and artistic casket as a present. Along with this gift, the friend sent a note insisting that the casket be placed only on the east or west side inside the house because its full beauty could be seen only when it faced east. Paying due respect to the wishes of his friend, Meyrink arranged for the casket to be put facing the right direction. But then he found that it did not match the other things in the room. Everything in the room seemed out of place, so he had to rearrange everything else. The table that the casket was placed on had to be moved to fit with everything else. The whole room had to be completely rearranged and as time went by, the whole house had to be renovated to harmonize with that room. Not only that, changes also had to be made in the garden outside the house!

This incident is very meaningful: the same thing happens in life. A single experience of truth or beauty or goodness transforms everything in life; you have to transform yourself because of it.

Someone who can make even a tiny part of his life peaceful and beautiful will soon experience his whole life becoming totally different. His higher parts start transforming the lower. The higher transforms the lower. And remember, a single drop of truth is more powerful than a whole ocean of lies.

77

Death only frightens someone who believes he is just the body. Entering a little deeper inside himself, he will find the place where there is no death at all. It is only through knowing that place of deathlessness that life is known.

Once, a princess became enamored with the body of a young sannyasin and the emperor asked him to marry her. The sannyasin said, "I am not, so who will marry her?" Taking this as an insult, the emperor ordered the sannyasin's head be cut off.

The sannyasin said, "My dear emperor, from the beginning I have had no connection with the body. You misunderstand. How can your sword separate what is already separate? But I am ready, and your sword is most welcome to cut off my so-called head, in the same way that the spring wind is making the flowers fall from the trees."

And actually it *was* spring and the flowers were falling from the trees. The emperor saw the falling flowers and saw also the eyes of the sannyasin, which were blissful in spite of the fact that he was facing death. He thought for a moment and then said, "It is meaningless to kill someone who is not afraid of death, and who accepts death just as if it were life. Even death cannot kill such a man."

Whatever can come to an end is not life. Whatever can be erased by death and burned by fire is not life. Those who take such things to be life will never really know life. They just live in death and that is why they are afraid of it. The sign of having found and known life is fearlessness of death.

What is the greatest mystical key to life? Whenever someone asks me this question, I reply: to die while alive.

An emperor wanted to honor a young man who had pleased him with his extraordinary service and bravery. An announcement was made that the greatest honor and position in the country would be bestowed upon him. However, it became known that the young man was not happy or satisfied with that. The emperor summoned him and asked, "What do you want? I am willing to give whatever you want. Your services are certainly greater than any reward."

The young man said: "Great emperor, my request is very small, and I only want that. I do not want wealth, or position or honor or status. I want peace of mind."

When the emperor heard this, he became silent for some time. Then he said, "How can I give what I don't have myself? Peace of mind – such wealth even I do not have." He took the man to a sage who had found peace and lived in the mountains and the young man expressed his request to the sage. The sage had an aura of ethereal peace and bliss about him, but the emperor noticed that, hearing the young man's request, the sage also became quiet, just as he had himself.

The emperor said to the sage, "It is also my request that you please bestow peace upon this young man. That is the reward he has asked me for his services and dedication. I myself am not at peace, so how could I give him peace? So I have brought him to you!"

The sage said, "Oh king, peace is not the kind of wealth that can be taken from, or given to, someone else.

You have to find it yourself. What you receive from others can also be taken away by others. And eventually death will take it away for sure. The only thing death can't take away is the wealth you find yourself, which you have not taken from anyone else. Peace is greater than death, which is why no one else can give it to you."

A mystic told me this story. Hearing it, I said: certainly death cannot snatch away peace. Only those who know how to die before death can find such peace.

Have you had the experience of death? If not, you are in the claws of death. The lack of peace that everyone is always feeling, is simply the anxiety of being in the hands of death. However, dear friend, there is a way to die before your death. He who lives in such a way that even while living he is not identified with life, comes to know death, and transcend death.

Truth is not found within the confines of words and scriptures. Actually, wherever there is a boundary, truth is not there. Truth is boundless, infinite. To know truth, you need to shatter the boundary of thoughts. The infinite is known only by becoming infinite. The moment consciousness is freed from the boundary of thoughts, it becomes infinite.

It is just as when an earthen pot is broken, the sky inside it merges with the infinite sky.

The sun had reached its peak in the sky. A beautiful swan was flying from one ocean to another. Tired from the long flight and the hot sun, it landed beside a well for a rest. Hardly had it settled than the voice of a frog called from inside the well, "Friend, who are you and where have you come from?"

The swan replied, "I am a very poor swan and my home is an ocean."

This was the first time the frog had met someone who knew the ocean. He asked, "How big is the ocean?"

The swan replied, "Endless."

Hearing this, the frog took a leap in the well and said, "This big?"

The swan started laughing and said, "Dear frog, no. The ocean is endlessly larger than that."

The frog took an even bigger jump and said, "This big?"

Finding the answer still in the negative, the frog leapt right across the well and said, "Must be this much! What could be bigger than this?" There was a glimmer of hope in his eyes and this time he was sure the answer wouldn't be negative.

But once again the swan said, "No, my friend! No. There is no way to measure the ocean using your well."

Hearing this, the frog laughed sarcastically and said, "Sir, there is a limit to lying. The ocean cannot be bigger than my world!"

What do I tell seekers of truth? I say: if you want to know the ocean of truth, come out of the well of your intellect. There just is no way to find truth through the intellect. Truth is immeasurable. Only he who breaks down all his barriers can find it. They are the only obstacle. The moment they disappear, not only does he know truth, he becomes one with it. To become one with it is to know it.

Are you a human being? Your humanity will be as high as your love is deep. And the higher your possessiveness, the lower will be your humanity. Love and possessiveness are two different directions in life. When love is total, possessiveness is absent. And love never visits those whose minds are full of possessiveness.

An empress left instructions for the following lines to be engraved on her tombstone after her death: "Immeasurable treasure is buried in this grave. Anyone who is destitute and helpless may dig up this grave and have it." Thousands of poor people and beggars passed the grave, but none was so poor that he would dig up the grave of a dead person for wealth.

A very old and destitute beggar had been living near the grave for many years, and he would point out the tombstone to every poor person who passed. Finally, someone arrived who was so poor that he could not prevent himself from digging up the grave. Who was he? He was an emperor who had just conquered the country where this grave lay. And the first thing he did was to dig up the grave; he wasted no time at all. But what did he find in that grave? Instead of immeasurable treasure, he found only a slab of stone with these words engraved on it, "Friend, are you a human being?" Certainly, how could someone who is human ever be prepared to disturb the dead? But what difference does that make to someone who is more than happy to kill the living for wealth?

When the emperor was leaving the grave, bitterly disappointed and humiliated, people saw the old beggar who lived near the grave laughing loudly. The beggar said, "I have been waiting for so many years, and finally I have met the most destitute, the weakest and poorest person on this earth!"

A man who has no love in his heart is poor, destitute, helpless and weak. Love is power, love is wealth, love is God. He who looks for a wealth other than love will one day find his own wealth asking him, "Are you a human being?"

"I am in the world and also not in the world" – only when someone can experience this does he experience the mystery of life. To be seen to be in the world is one thing, but to be in the world is something else altogether. To be seen to be in the world is a physical phenomena, to *be* in the world is a spiritual calamity. As long as there is life, the body will stay in the world. But he who longs to know that other life – which never ends – will have to distance himself from this world.

A sannyasin once heard that the emperor of the country had become enlightened. He was surprised beyond words – how was it possible that someone who had not renounced anything could find godliness? He went to the capital and was a guest of the emperor. He saw him wearing precious clothes, eating delicious food served in gold dishes – and in the night he saw him enjoying music, festivity and dance. When the sannyasin saw all this, he was even more skeptical about whether the emperor was enlightened. He was utterly astonished! Somehow the night passed, but he could not sleep because of all this doubt and worry.

Early in the morning, the emperor invited him to join him for a bath in the river. They both entered the river and had only just begun to bathe when the calm of the atmosphere was shattered by piercing shrieks. Everywhere there were cries of "Fire! Fire! Fire!" The palace that stood silently majestic on the bank of the river was ablaze, engulfed in huge flames, and the flames were rapidly approaching the river bank.

Suddenly, the sannyasin found himself running up the

steps of the river bank to save his saffron robe. He totally forgot that the emperor was with him. When he turned to look, he found the emperor still standing in the river and saying, "O monk, even if the whole kingdom is burned down, still nothing of mine will be burned." The name of the emperor was Janak and the monk was Shukdev.

People ask me, "What is yoga?" I tell them it is the sense of remaining undisturbed. Live in the world, but do not belong to it. When consciousness is untouched by what is outside, it settles in itself.

Remember, you will be recognized not by what you have, but by what you are. That alone is your wealth, and that alone is you. If you have awareness of that, you have taken care of everything.

There is a story about an old, blind mystic who was standing in the middle of the road when the royal entourage was about to pass by.

First came the foot soldiers whose job was to clear the road ahead of the entourage, so it could pass unhindered. They pushed the old man, telling him, "You fool, get out of the way. Are you blind? Can't you see that the royal carriage is coming?"

The old man laughed and said, "Because of that." And he remained standing in the same place.

Then another group of soldiers came, on horseback. They said, "Get out of the way, the royal carriage is coming."

The old man remained standing where he was and said, "Because of that."

Then the king's ministers came. They did not say anything to the old man and, quietly avoiding him, led their horses around the other way. The fakir repeated again, "Because of that."

Then the royal carriage came. The king got down from his carriage and touched the feet of the old man. The fakir started laughing and said, "Has the king arrived? Because of that." Then the carriage went on its way.

The people who had seen the old man laughing and had heard him repeating "Because of that," asked him why he had said it.

He replied, "Everyone is what they are because of their behavior."

I am seen in everything I think, everything I speak, everything I do. And the person who can constantly look at and examine all these aspects of himself continues to rise higher and higher. Who is there who wants to knowingly remain on the lowest rung?

Tensions and dilemmas in life arise from the conflict between "I" and "no-I." That is the basis of anxiety and unhappiness. Whosoever transcends this duality enters godliness.

A young man asked, "What shall I do to find godliness?" I said: make "I" either a zero or the whole. He did not understand, so I had to tell him a story:

Once, two mystics met. Hundreds of their disciples were also there. It was well known that the two mystics held totally opposing views. The first mystic asked the other, "Friend, what have you found from your life's search? As far as I am concerned, I have lost my I. It gradually weakened and now it is totally erased. Not a single trace of it remains. Now I am not, only 'that' is. Everything is, but I am not. Everything is the will of existence. And to just go on flowing in its current – to just go on living as nothingness – what bliss! Whatever I had to find, I have found, and whatever I had to become, I have become. Ah! How much power there is in letting go of the I, how much peace and beauty there is in letting go of the I!"

Hearing this, the second mystic said: "Friend, I have simply become I. Now only I am, nothing else is there. I am all. Whatever is outside of I, is simply not. *Aham brahmasmi*, I am the whole. It is I who moves the moon and the stars, it is I who makes and unmakes creation. This whole game of creation is nothing but my will. And friend, in this triumph of the I, there is such bliss, such peace, such beauty!"

Listening to this conversation, the disciples of both

mystics were greatly astonished. And they were even more puzzled when, as they were parting from each other, both mystics embraced and said, "How identical are our experiences! In spite of traveling such opposite paths, we have arrived at the same truth."

If I is reduced to zero, it becomes the whole. Or, if I is expanded to become the whole, it becomes zero. Zero and the whole are one and the same thing. He who moves from zero reaches nirvana, the ultimate nothing. And he who moves from the whole arrives at *brahman*, the absolute whole. But aren't nirvana and *brahman* two names of the same state?

In the name of God, fantasies are taught. But realization of truth does not happen through imagination; it only happens after all imagination has been dropped. He who lives in imagination is in a dream. He sees what he wants to see, and not what actually is.

A Sufi mystic was once invited to a school where special emphasis was put on teaching children how to concentrate. Around ten or twelve children were brought to him and each was told to concentrate on a white screen with all the power of their minds and then to say what they saw on it.

One small child was staring, and after a long look said, "I see a roseflower." Even his eyes showed that he was seeing a roseflower. Each child said something different; they were just seeing their own imaginings. But don't many older people also just see projections of their imagination, the same as those children? In fact, he who doesn't rise above imagination remains immature. Maturity is reached only by seeing without imagining.

Then another child, who had been staring for a very long time, said, "Nothing. I do not see anything." He was asked to look again, but even after a second look he said, "I am sorry. What can I do? There is nothing there!" His teachers were disappointed with him and sent him away, saying he lacked concentration. They were very happy with the children who had seen something. But in fact the boy who was a failure in their eyes was nearer the truth than all the others. He was seeing the reality.

Truth is not man's imagination – neither is godliness.

He who sees through his imagination sees unreality. Imagination is not meditation; it is absolutely the opposite state to meditation. Where imagination ends, meditation begins. What is known, not through imagination but through meditation, is truth.

I once went to a village and some people there asked me, "Does godliness exist? We would like to find it." I told them: nothing exists *except* godliness – everything is godliness. But those who are full of "I" cannot realize it. To realize it, the condition is that they must first lose themselves.

Once, there was a king who wanted to experience godliness. He went to an ashram and was told, "Renounce everything you have. Then it is easy to experience godliness." The king went away, renounced everything, and returned to the ashram. He had renounced his kingdom and distributed all his wealth to the poor and needy. He came like a beggar. But seeing him, the head of the ashram said, "Friend, you have brought everything with you!" The king could not understand what he meant.

He was given the job of cleaning and throwing away all the garbage of the ashram. The others felt this was a little harsh, but the abbot said, "He is not yet ready to experience truth, and it is essential to be ready."

After a few days, they again approached the abbot with a request to relieve the king of this hard task, so he said, "Let us test him."

The next day, when the king was carrying the garbage bin on his head to empty it outside the village, someone bumped into him. He told the man who had bumped into him, "Sir, I don't think you would have been so blind fifteen days ago!"

When the abbot heard about this, he said, "Didn't I tell you that the time hasn't yet come? He is still the same old person."

A few days later, someone else bumped into the king. This time he just stared and didn't say anything, but his eyes said everything there was to say!

When the abbot heard about this he said, "How easy it is to let go of wealth, but how difficult to let go of the ego."

The incident happened a third time. That time the king merely picked up all the garbage that had fallen, put it back in the bin and went on his way as if nothing had happened at all. That day, the abbot said, "Now he is ready. He who is willing to erase himself is worthy of experiencing godliness."

If you long for truth, then let go of your ego. There is no greater lie than "I." To drop that is sannyas: "I," is to be renounced, not the world. Because, actually, the sense of I *is* the world.

86

Someone asked, "What is fear?" and I said: ignorance. Fear is not knowing yourself because he who does not know himself knows only death.

Where there is self-realization, enlightenment, there is life and only life; there is God and only God. And to be in God is to be without fear. Before that, all fearlessness is false.

The sun is about to set and Mohammed and a companion are hiding behind a rock; the enemy is in hot pursuit and their lives are in danger. They can hear the sound of the enemy's army coming closer and closer with each passing moment.

Mohammed's companion says, "Now death seems certain, there are too many of them and we are just two!" His alarm and fear of death are quite natural: they may have only a short while to live.

But Mohammed starts laughing when he hears this and says, "Two? Are we only two? No, not two, but three: I, you and God." Mohammed's eyes are peaceful and there is no fear in his heart; there is no death in eyes where God dwells – just as there is no darkness where there is light. Certainly, if there is soul, if there is God, then there is no death. Because in God there can only be life. And if there is no God, then everything is death. What possible connection can there be between death and life? The moment you know life, death disappears. It is ignorance of life that is the fear of death.

Religiousness is a way to rise above fear; it is the bridge that connects to life.

Those who think that religiousness is based in fear either don't understand religiousness at all, or what they understand to be religiousness is not. Fear is irreligiousness – because what can be irreligious other than ignorance of life!

87

What I see is that most people are clothes and nothing but clothes! It is as if there is nothing to them, except their clothes. For a man who does not know himself, whether he exists, or not, is all the same. And those who are clothes and nothing but clothes, am I to call them alive? No, my friend, they are dead and their clothes are their graves.

An extremely naive and simple sort of man once asked a mystic, "What is death? And how will I know that I have died?"

The mystic said, "Friend, when your clothes have become tattered and worn out, know that you have died."

From that day on, the man put all his energy into taking care of the clothes he was wearing. He even stopped taking baths because bathing would mean removing his clothes again and again, washing them and putting them on, which would just make them weaker. His worry was quite justified to him because his clothes were his very life! But clothes are, after all, clothes, and eventually they became torn and worn out. Seeing them destroyed like that, the man started weeping inconsolably because he thought his death had come. Seeing him weeping bitterly, people asked him what had happened. He replied, "I have died; my clothes have become torn and worn out."

This incident seems highly impossible and unimaginable, but I ask you: isn't everyone just like this, that when their clothes are destroyed they think that they are destroyed? What else is the body except clothing? He who thinks himself to be only the body is taking his clothing to be his life. Then, when the clothes are tattered and worn out, he feels his life coming to an end. But life has no beginning and no end.

Only the body has a birth, and only the body dies. What is inside us is not a body. It is life. He who does not know it is surrounded by death, even though he is alive. And he who knows it finds life even in death.

88

Someone asked, "What is heaven and hell?" I said: we ourselves.

Once a disciple said to his master, "I want to know what heaven and hell are like."

His master said, "Close your eyes and see." The disciple closed his eyes and went into a peaceful void. Then the master said, "Now see heaven." And then he said, "And now hell."

When the disciple opened his eyes, they were full of amazement and the master asked, "What did you see?"

The disciple replied, "I didn't see any of the things people usually say are in heaven. I saw no golden palaces or flowing rivers of nectar none of that was there. And neither was there anything in hell. There were no raging fires, nor screaming people being burned and tortured. What does it mean? Did I see heaven and hell, or not?"

His master laughed and said, "You have certainly seen heaven and hell, but as for golden palaces, rivers of nectar, blazing fires and the screams of people being tortured, you have to bring all those things there yourself. They are not there. What we bring ourselves is what we find. We are heaven, we are hell."

Whatsoever a person is inside, is what he finds outside too. The outside is just a projection of the inner. If there is heaven inside, heaven is outside also. And if there is hell inside, then hell is outside also. Everything is hidden inside you.

89

It is not what the scriptures say that is true, but what love says. Is there any scripture greater than love?

Once, Moses was passing a riverbank. He heard a shepherd who was talking to himself. The shepherd was saying, "O God! I have heard many things about you – that you are very beautiful, very lovely, and very kind. If you ever happen to come to me, I will give you my own clothes to wear and protect you day and night from wild animals. I will bathe you in the river every day and give you nice things to eat – I will give you milk, bread and butter. You know how much I love you, God. Please reveal yourself to me. If I can see you just once, I will give you everything that belongs to me."

When Moses heard all this, he told the shepherd, "You fool! What are you saying? You will protect God who is the protector of everyone? You will give him food and make him wear your dirty clothes? You will bathe holy God in the river? You are trying to attract the one who owns everything by saying you will give him everything *you* own?"

When the shepherd heard Moses, he shook with sadness and remorse. His eyes filled with tears and he immediately knelt down on the ground to beg God's forgiveness.

But Moses had hardly moved a few steps when he heard a voice coming from the innermost depths of his heart, "You idiot! What have you done? I sent you so that you could bring my beloveds closer to me; on the contrary, you have sent one of my beloveds away from me!"

"Where shall we seek God?" I say: in love. And if there is love, then remember, he is in a stone also.

90

Discoveries! Discoveries! Discoveries! How many discoveries are made every day! And yet, day by day, life becomes more and more of an anguish. To explain hell, you don't have to use your imagination anymore. It is enough to point to the world and say, "This is what hell is like." And what has caused this state? The cause is that man himself has remained undiscovered.

I see that man has opened the door to outer space and is preparing for the far-off journey into the skies. But, isn't it surprising that the doors to his inner self have remained closed? He has totally forgotten about the journey he can take to his own inner self. I ask: is this a gain or a loss? Even if he were to find everything else by losing his self, what value and meaning would that have? Even victory over the whole universe cannot heal the wound of losing that small point which is he himself, which is the center of his very existence.

It was only last night that someone asked, "What shall I do and what will I attain?" I said: find your self. Always remember that whatever you do, it should help you to find your self. Anything that takes you away from your self is irreligion. And anything that brings you to your self is what I have known to be religion.

Even if there is a tiny flame of light inside you, it defeats the darkness of the whole world. And, if there is darkness at your center, even a million suns in the outer sky will not be able to eliminate it.

My message is very short: Love. Love everyone. And **91** remember, no message is, or ever can be, greater than this.

I have heard...

One evening in a town, a funeral procession was passing, with many people accompanying the dead body. And it was not as if it was a king's funeral – an ordinary beggar had died. People were amazed to see so many people come to say good-bye to a penniless beggar.

The maidservant of a large mansion ran in and told her mistress, "A beggar has died and gone to heaven."

The mistress, laughing at such an authoritative declaration that the dead person had gone to heaven, asked her, "Did you see him entering heaven?"

The maidservant replied, "Yes certainly, madam! It is so easy to understand. You see, all the people accompanying the funeral were weeping bitterly. Doesn't that prove that the departed soul left a lasting imprint of love on the minds of the people he lived amongst?"

The imprints of love – as I think on it, I see that the imprints of love are also the very steps to the door of God. Is there any way to reach God except through love? What can be proof of attaining godliness, except that someone has found love on this earth? What is love in this world, is God in the other world.

Love unites. That is why love is the ultimate experience. How can something which divides ever be the ultimate experience? When the experiencer is separate from the object of experiencing, there is ignorance.

92 Someone asked, "Is man good or evil?" I replied: by nature he is good. Let this fact become more and more rooted inside because nothing is more important than this for growth in life.

There is a story of a king, who gave three different punishments to three courtiers for the same crime. The first, he sent to prison for a few years. The second, he exiled from the country. But to the third he merely said, "I am really surprised – I never expected something like this from you."

Do you know the effect these three different punishments had? The first man was very remorseful, the second man too, and so was the third, but all three had quite different reasons for their remorse. All three were unhappy because of the insult and disgrace, but while the first two found themselves disgraced in the eyes of other people, the third was disgraced in his own eyes.

This is a very big difference. The first man soon made friends with the other prisoners and the staff and lived quite happily in prison. The second man, after leaving the country, started a flourishing business and soon found himself making a lot of money. But what could the third man do? His feelings of repentance were very deep because he had been disgraced in his own eyes. He had been acknowledged as good and so goodness had been expected of him. And it was precisely that which began to prick at him like a thorn. And this inner prick pushed him to rehabilitate himself. His transformation started because he himself began to long for what had been expected of him.

Trust in goodness is the beginning of goodness arising. Trust in truth acts like rain, making the seed of truth sprout and flourish. And trust in beauty acts like a sunrise that awakens the beauty which was asleep.

Remember, never let your eyes see evil in anyone's nature because there is nothing more evil than that. Seeing evil in others will only reinforce it in them. Evil is no one's nature, it is an accident. That is why someone who finds evil in himself feels humiliated in his own eyes. The sun does not become a cloud just because it has been temporarily covered by clouds. Never, under any circumstances, put your trust in clouds. If your attention is on the sun, the sun will rise that much sooner.

93

People who have become religious out of fear deceive themselves that they have become religious. Fear and religiousness are opposites. Fearlessness is the only door to religiousness.

Someone was asking me, "You say godliness is inside, but I do not see anything in there." I said to him: friend, you are quite right in what you say. But not seeing it does not mean it is absent. If there are clouds, the sun is not seen; nor is it seen if the eyes are closed. I have looked into thousands of eyes and searched thousands of hearts, but I see nothing but fear. And remember, where there is fear, you cannot see truth. Fear is like dark clouds that cover the sun. And the smoke of fear prevents the eyes from opening. He who wants to find truth must first get rid of fear. You have to renounce all your fears if you want to see the ultimate reality. A mind trembling with fear can never be calm, and that is why it can't even see what lies close to it, cannot see what you yourself are. Fear is trembling, fearlessness is stillness. Fear is instability, fearlessness is *samadhi*, a profound rootedness in your being.

What does fear do to the mind? – the same thing blindness does to the eyes. There is no place for fear in the search for truth. Remember, not even fear of the ultimate has any place. Fear is fear, it doesn't matter what the fear is about. Total fearlessness opens the eyes to truth.

Don't ever be miserly when choosing an ideal. It should be the highest. Actually, anything less than truth is not an ideal at all. An ideal is the prophecy of what you will ultimately become one day. It is a declaration of the ultimate expression of your self-nature.

Many people come to see me, from morning to evening. I always ask them: where does your soul lie? Suddenly, they cannot understand. Then I tell them that the soul of each person lies in his life's ideal. What he wants to be, what he wants to attain, is where his soul lies. And what he doesn't want to be, doesn't want to attain, has no life.

Where we put our soul is in our own hands. And where a man places his soul – high or low – affects whether his life current moves upward or down. Your eyes will be fixed on the place where your soul is, and with each in and out breath, your remembrance will keep running back to it. Gradually, the seeds of your thoughts will be sown onto that path on which your memory races.

Thoughts are the seeds of action. What is a thought today sprouts and becomes your action tomorrow, whenever there is a suitable opportunity. That is why the most important thing in life is to choose the right place for your soul. Those who live without making this choice are like boats put to sea with no idea of a destination. Boats like this are as good as sunk. The lives of those who drift about in unintelligence and unawareness will revolve around just their bodily desires. They will never be able to know any truth higher than the body. They remain deprived of that ultimate treasure which lies hidden within them.

Wake up from unintelligence and unawareness! Open your eyes and look at the tall, snow-capped, mountain peaks of life that are shining in the sunlight, beckoning to you. If you can give birth to the longing in your heart to reach them, they are not far away at all.

When I hear people debating about truth, I am always surprised. The people debating are certainly ignorant because you cannot debate truth. Truth does not have any camp or position; all camps and sides belong to ignorance. Truth is without camps, it is impartial. Those who get caught up in debatable ideologies and prejudices create walls between themselves and the truth by their own hands. My advice is: let go of all thoughts and be in a state of non-thinking. Let go of all positions and be without opinions. It is only in this way that the light which reveals truth is available.

Once, a type of animal previously unknown was brought to a pitch dark and dingy cage. Many people came to see it and, since they couldn't see it in the pitch dark, everyone felt it with their hands and tried to make out what it looked like. Someone said, "This animal resembles one of the pillars in the royal palace."

Another retorted, "No, it is like a big fan." A third person said something else, and a fourth something else again. Everyone who was there had their own version of how the animal really looked. This generated a heated, antagonistic discussion. Of course the reality was one, but the opinions were many. Actually, it was an elephant that was tied up in that dark cage, but each person was claiming his idea to be right, basing his decision on the part of the elephant he had touched. If each had just held a small lamp in his hand, all this needless controversy could have been avoided!

What was their problem? Their problem was simply a lack of light. And this is everyone's problem. The truth of life can only be seen in the light of *samadhi*, no-mind. Those who touch it with thoughts find only debatable opinions, not the real truth.

If you want to know truth, look for light, not theories. The question is not of thoughts, but of light. And the light exists inside each of us. A person who frees himself from the turmoil of thoughts finds the eternal flame which has always been burning inside him.

96

I see people trembling with fear. They live their entire lives in a hellish trembling because they know only the wealth that is outside them. And as their wealth increases on the outside, so does their fear – although they run after wealth to get rid of fear! Alas! If they only knew that there is another wealth, which is inside everyone... He who discovers this wealth becomes fearless.

It was a no-moon evening. The sun was setting in the west and the darkness of night was approaching. An old hermit was passing through a forest with one of his young disciples. Seeing the darkness approaching, he asked the young man: "Night is coming and this is a dense forest. Is there anything to fear or worry about on the path ahead?" Hearing this, the young hermit was quite astonished – why should a hermit have any fear?

Fear is never outside, its roots are always some where inside. As the evening was settling, the old hermit handed over his bag to the young man and went for his toilet and bath. He looked worried and fearful as he handed over the bag, so as soon as he went away, the young man looked inside and saw that there was a brick of gold there! He stopped wondering – he had found the reason for the fear.

When the old hermit returned, he took his bag from the young man and they resumed their journey. As the night deepened and the lonely forest path was covered in dense darkness, the old hermit again asked the same question. Hearing it, the young man laughed and said, "Please, you can be fearless now. We have no reason to be afraid now!"

The old hermit looked at him in surprise and said, "The forest hasn't ended!"

The young man answered: "Not the forest, but the fear has ended. I threw it into the well back there!" Hearing this, the old man nervously looked inside his bag. And found a brick of stone instead of a brick of gold. For a moment, he felt as if his heart had stopped, but the very next moment he woke up; that no-moon night became a full-moon night for him In bliss from the light he had seen, he started to dance. He had glimpsed an extraordinary truth. That night they slept in the same forest, but there was no darkness, nor any fear.

There is a difference between the two kinds of wealth. The fortune which is collected on the outside is actually not wealth at all. It is better to call it misfortune. True fortune is found only by discovering the self. That which creates fear is misfortune and that which creates fearlessness, I call the only true wealth.

97

Some young men asked me, "What is sin?" I replied: unconsciousness.

Actually, it is impossible to commit any sin consciously. That is why I say virtue is any act that you can only do with full awareness. And sin is what you can only do with unconsciousness, unawareness.

One dark night, a young man entered a hermit's hut. He said, "I want to become your disciple."

The hermit replied, "You are most welcome. Everyone is always welcome at the doorstep of truth."

The young man was taken aback a little and said, "But I have a lot of shortcomings – I am a great sinner."

Hearing this, the hermit laughed and said, "When existence accepts you, then who am I to refuse? I also accept you, along with all your sins."

The young man said: "But I gamble, I am a drunkard, I am not a good character."

The hermit said, "None of these things make any difference. But look! I have accepted you, will you also accept me? When you do these things you call sins, would you remember to at least not do them in my presence? Can I expect at least this much from you?" The young man assured the hermit on that count. To have at least this much respect for the master was natural.

But when he returned a few days later and the master asked him how his sins were going, he laughed and said, "The moment I start becoming unconscious about them, I see your eyes in front of me and I wake up. Your presence wakes me up. And it is impossible to fall into a ditch awake!"

As I see it, sin and virtue are not mere actions. Actually, they are indications of whether we are asleep or awake. He who fights with sin, or wants to do some virtuous act, is sadly mistaken. It is not a question of doing or not doing something. The question is of being or not being something inside. And if there is wakefulness inside – if there is consciousness, if there is self-awareness – only then you *are*. Otherwise, the ease that thieves have when the master of a house is asleep, is also available to sins when the inner master is asleep.

98

Man has to constantly renew himself, each and every moment. He has to give birth to himself. Those who don't know this art of constantly being reborn should be aware that they have died long ago.

Last night, some people came to see me. They asked, "What is religion?" I said to them: religion is the art of man being reborn as God. Man possesses the power both for self-destruction and for self-creation; he can destroy himself or create himself. And he is free to choose either option. That is his responsibility to himself.

His love for himself is the beginning of his love for the world. The more he can love himself, the more he closes the path to his self-destruction. And whatever is suicidal for him, is irreligious when it concerns others.

Lack of love toward his own being and its potential growth is what becomes sin. So the source of sin and virtue, of good and evil, of religiousness and irreligiousness, exists within his self – not in some God, or in some other world.

Transformation comes from the intense realization of this truth, which wakes us up to the responsibility inherent in being a human being. Then life is not simply living; then life becomes full of sublime elements and we get absorbed in constantly creating our self. Those who have this realization continue to give birth to themselves in higher levels of consciousness. It is in this ongoing creation that the beauty of life is found. Life becomes full of music and poetry and gradually rises above the darkness and the fog of the valleys, making the eyes of our hearts capable of seeing the sun.

Life is an art. And man is both the artist of his life and the instrument of that art. He finds himself to be exactly how he creates himself. Remember that man is not born ready-made; when we are born, we are all like unhewn stones. And we are the creators of whatever ugly or beautiful statues we become.

99

There is no contentment other than godliness. Nothing but that can fill your heart.

A huge crowd had gathered in front of a royal palace; a wandering mystic had begged alms from the emperor. The emperor told him, "Ask for anything and it shall be granted." It was the royal custom to grant anything asked for by the first beggar of the day.

The mystic held out his small begging bowl and said, "Just fill this with gold coins."

"That will be easy thing to do," thought the emperor.

But when the gold coins were put in the bowl, it was found that it was impossible to fill it. The bowl was magical. The more gold coins put into it, the emptier it became.

Seeing the emperor looking worried, the mystic said, "If you can't fill it, just say so. It doesn't matter, I will go empty-handed. The worst that can happen is that people will say the emperor could not fulfill his promise." The emperor emptied his whole treasury, but the bowl remained empty. He put everything he owned into that bowl, but the bowl just refused to be filled.

Finally, the emperor said to the mystic, "O monk, your bowl is not an ordinary one. It is beyond my means to fill it. But what is the secret of this unique bowl?"

The mystic laughed and said, "There is no special secret. It has been made from man's heart." Don't you know that man's heart can never be filled? No matter what you fill it with – wealth, rank, knowledge – it will always remain empty because it is not designed to be filled with those things. It is because of ignorance of this truth that the more man gets, the more destitute he becomes. The desires of the heart are never satisfied, no matter what man gets, because the heart is designed to be filled with godliness.

You want peace? You want contentment? Then let your will declare, "The only thing I want is godliness."

Where is God? People searching for God come to me **100** and I tell them that God is present everywhere, in every moment. There is no need to go anywhere to look for it. Wake up – and see. And whatever you see when you wake up, is nothing but God.

The Sufi poet Hafiz was in his master's hermitage. Many other disciples were there too. One night, the master asked all the disciples to sit silently in meditation. Around midnight, he called in a whisper: "Hafiz!" Hearing this, Hafiz at once stood up and went to him. The master said what he wanted to say to him. After some time, the master called somebody else by name. But it was Hafiz who went. The master called out like this ten times, but each time only Hafiz went because all the others were sleeping.

God is also calling out to everyone, each and every moment. From all directions, in all possible ways, it is the voice of God that resounds. But we are asleep. Only he who is awake hears that voice; only he who is awake finds God. That is why I say don't worry about God. Worrying about it is futile; worry about waking yourself up. Whatever we know in sleep is only a distorted form of God. This distorted experience is your world. The moment you wake up, what you find is God.

God is all around. Actually, only God exists, nothing else. But we are dreaming, so that which is, is not seen. Let go of dreams. Leaving dreams, not the world, is what sannyas, or surrender, is. And he who drops dreams finds that he himself is God.

About Osho

Osho defies categorization. His thousands of talks cover everything from the individual quest for meaning to the most urgent social and political issues facing society today. Osho's books are not written but are transcribed from audio and video recordings of his extemporaneous talks to international audiences. As he puts it, "So remember: whatever I am saying is not just for you... I am talking also for the future generations."

Osho has been described by *The Sunday Times* in London as one of the "1000 Makers of the 20th Century" and by American author Tom Robbins as "the most dangerous man since Jesus Christ." *Sunday Mid-Day* (India) has selected Osho as one of ten people – along with Gandhi, Nehru and Buddha – who have changed the destiny of India.

About his own work Osho has said that he is helping to create the conditions for the birth of a new kind of human being. He often characterizes this new human being as "Zorba the Buddha" – capable both of enjoying the earthy pleasures of a Zorba the Greek and the silent serenity of a Gautama the Buddha.

Running like a thread through all aspects of Osho's talks and meditations is a vision that encompasses both the timeless wisdom of all ages past and the highest potential of today's (and tomorrow's) science and technology.

Osho is known for his revolutionary contribution to the science of inner transformation, with an approach to meditation that acknowledges the accelerated pace of contemporary life. His unique OSHO Active Meditations™ are designed to first release the accumulated stresses of body and mind, so that it is then easier to take an experience of stillness and thought-free relaxation into daily life.

Two autobiographical works by the author are available:
Autobiography of a Spiritually Incorrect Mystic,
St Martins Press, New York (book and eBook)
Glimpses of a Golden Childhood,
OSHO Media International, Pune, India (book and eBook)

OSHO International Meditation Resort

Location
Located 100 miles southeast of Mumbai in the thriving modern city of Pune, India, the OSHO International Meditation Resort is a holiday destination with a difference. The Meditation Resort is spread over 28 acres of spectacular gardens in a beautiful tree-lined residential area.

Uniqueness
Each year the Meditation Resort welcomes thousands of people from more than 100 countries. The unique campus provides an opportunity for a direct personal experience of a new way of living – with more awareness, relaxation, celebration and creativity. A great variety of around-the-clock and around-the-year program options are available. Doing nothing and just relaxing is one of them!

All programs are based on the OSHO vision of "Zorba the Buddha" – a qualitatively new kind of human being who is able *both* to participate creatively in everyday life *and* to relax into silence and meditation.

OSHO Meditations
A full daily schedule of meditations for every type of person includes methods that are active and passive, traditional and revolutionary, and in particular the OSHO Active Meditations™. The meditations take place

in what must be the world's largest meditation hall, the OSHO Auditorium.

OSHO Multiversity

Individual sessions, courses and workshops cover everything from creative arts to holistic health, personal transformation, relationship and life transition, work-as-meditation, esoteric sciences, and the "Zen" approach to sports and recreation. The secret of the OSHO Multiversity's success lies in the fact that all its programs are combined with meditation, supporting the understanding that as human beings we are far more than the sum of our parts.

OSHO Basho Spa

The luxurious Basho Spa provides for leisurely open-air swimming surrounded by trees and tropical green. The uniquely styled, spacious Jacuzzi, the saunas, gym, tennis courts...all these are enhanced by their stunningly beautiful setting.

Cuisine

A variety of different eating areas serve delicious Western, Asian and Indian vegetarian food – most of it organically grown especially for the Meditation Resort. Breads and cakes are baked in the resort's own bakery.

Night life

There are many evening events to choose from – dancing being at the top of the list! Other activities include full-moon meditations beneath the stars, variety shows, music performances and meditations for daily life.

Or you can just enjoy meeting people at the Plaza Café, or walking in the nighttime serenity of the gardens of this fairytale environment.

Facilities
You can buy all your basic necessities and toiletries in the Galleria. The Multimedia Gallery sells a large range of OSHO media products. There is also a bank, a travel agency and a Cyber Café on-campus. For those who enjoy shopping, Pune provides all the options, ranging from traditional and ethnic Indian products to all of the global brand-name stores.

Accommodation
You can choose to stay in the elegant rooms of the OSHO Guesthouse, or for longer stays opt for one of the OSHO Living-In program packages. Additionally there is a plentiful variety of nearby hotels and serviced apartments.

www.osho.com/meditationresort
www.osho.com/guesthouse
www.osho.com/livingin

For More Information

www.**OSHO**.com

a comprehensive multi-language website including a magazine, OSHO Books, OSHO Talks in audio and video formats, the OSHO Library text archive in English and Hindi and extensive information about OSHO Meditations. You will also find the program schedule of the OSHO Multiversity and information about the OSHO International Meditation Resort.

http://OSHO.com/AllAboutOSHO
http://OSHO.com/Resort
http://OSHO.com/Shop
http://www.youtube.com/OSHO
http://www.Twitter.com/OSHO
http://www.facebook.com/pages/OSHO.International

To contact OSHO International Foundation:
www.osho.com/oshointernational,
oshointernational@oshointernational.com